A Gabriel Marcel Reader

A Gabriel Marcel Reader

Gabriel Marcel

Edited and Introduced by
Brendan Sweetman

ST. AUGUSTINE'S PRESS
South Bend, Indiana

Manufactured in the United States of America

1 2 3 4 5 6   16 15 14 13 12 11

Library of Congress Cataloging in Publication Data
Marcel, Gabriel, 1889–1973.
    [Selections. English. 2011]
    A Gabriel Marcel reader / Gabriel Marcel; edited and introduced by
    Brendan Sweetman.
       p. cm.
    Includes bibliographical references and index.
    ISBN 978-1-58731-326-4 (paperbound: alk. paper)
    I. Sweetman, Brendan. II. Title.
    B2430.M252E5 2011   194 – dc22   2011001392

1. Excerpts from Gabriel Marcel, *Tragic Wisdom and Beyond,* trans. S. Jolin and P. McCormick, copyright © 1973 by Northwestern University Press.

2. Excerpts from Gabriel Marcel, *Searchings*, copyright © 1967 by The Missionary Society of St. Paul the Apostle in the State of New York. Paulist Press, Inc., New York/Rahway, NJ. Reprinted by permission of Paulist Press, Inc. www. paulistpress.com

3. Excepts from Gabriel Marcel, *The Philosophy of Existentialism*, copyright © 1956, 1984 Philosophical Library. All rights reserved. Reprinted by arrangement with Kensington Publishing Corp. www. kensingtonbooks.com

∞ The paper used in this publication meets the minimum requirements of the American National Standard for Information Sciences - Permanence of Paper for Printed Materials, ANSI Z39.48 – 1984.

ST. AUGUSTINE'S PRESS
www.staugustine.net

For Gerry, Eric and Denise

TABLE OF CONTENTS

ABBREVIATIONS

The following abbreviations for the titles of Marcel's major works are used to identify the sources of the various selections in this book. Full details may be found in the Bibliography.

MBI	—	*The Mystery of Being*, Vol. I
MBII	—	*The Mystery of Being*, Vol. II
CF	—	*Creative Fidelity*
BH	—	*Being and Having*
HV	—	*Homo Viator*
TWB	—	*Tragic Wisdom and Beyond*
PE	—	*The Philosophy of Existentialism*
EBHD	—	*The Existential Background of Human Dignity*
MJ	—	*Metaphysical Journal*
MMS	—	*Man Against Mass Society*
P&I	—	*Presence and Immortality*
S	—	*Searchings*

INTRODUCTION

French existentialist philosopher Gabriel Marcel (1883–1973) is one of the most influential thinkers of the twentieth century. The themes of Marcel's philosophy, which are developed with a blend of realism, concreteness, and common sense, continue to be relevant for the plight of humanity in the twentieth first century. Marcel's thought is attractive because he emphasizes a number of significant ideas that have been influential in contemporary thinking in both philosophy and theology: the attempt to safeguard the dignity and integrity of the human person by emphasizing the inadequacy of the materialistic life and the unavoidable human need for transcendence; the inability of philosophy to capture the profundity and depth of key human experiences, and so the need to find a deeper kind of reflection; the importance of the experience of intersubjectivity, which Marcel believes is at the root of human fulfillment, and which also finds expression in the transcendent dimension of human experience, a dimension that cannot be denied without loss, and that often gives meaning to our most profound experiences. Marcel is also one of the few contemporary thinkers who manages to do justice to the subjectivity and individuality of the human person, while at the same time avoiding the relativism and skepticism that has tended to accompany these notions, and that has plagued contemporary philosophy after Heidegger. He is also important because he makes an unwavering effort to challenge the moral relativism and spiritual nihilism of his French rival, Jean Paul Sartre, and of other representative existentialist philosophers.

Marcel's books have been often out of print in recent times, and this Reader is an attempt to bring together in one place a broad range of selections from his work organized around the major themes, so that a new generation of readers will have the opportunity to benefit from his insights. All of his important ideas are introduced here ranging from his unique conception of philosophy; to his original approach to epistemology and the nature of knowledge; to his view on the nature of the human person, including the idea of being-in-a-situation and the importance of the "context" that the subject lives in for the subject's ideas and experiences; to his approach to religious themes, including the issues of the rationality of religious belief, the question of God's existence, and our longing for the transcendent; to his "concrete approaches" of fidelity, hope, love and faith. There are also selections in which he discusses some of his misgivings about the direction of contemporary culture, especially the effects of technology, and in which we see his reactions to various other philosophers and philosophies. My hope is that this wide-ranging, rich selection of readings will whet readers' appetites for sampling more of Marcel, and will send us back to the original works for a more comprehensive look at the ideas of this extraordinary French thinker.

Marcel was born in Paris in 1889, an only child, and his mother died when he was four years old. His father, a diplomat, later married Marcel's aunt. His father was a lapsed Catholic, who later became an agnostic; his aunt was nominally a liberal Protestant. As a result, Marcel received little or no religious training or upbringing. He enrolled in the Sorbonne and earned a *license en philosophie* in 1907. He married Jacqueline Boegner in 1918, and they later adopted a son.

Marcel's various philosophical reflections in his early works, *Journal métaphysique* (*Metaphysical Journal*, first published in French in 1927), and *Être et avoir* (*Being and Having*, 1935), laid the seeds for his conversion to Catholicism. He came to see that his main ideas, although developed within an existentialist framework, were nevertheless compatible with (and indeed later came to *require*) a religious view of the world. In 1929, Marcel converted to Catholicism, at the age of thirty nine. It is interesting to note, but not surprising, that his conversion did not significantly change his philosophy, although he inevitably came to explore the nature of the transcendent more fully in his works.

Marcel did not hold a formal third-level position as a philosopher, but rather worked as a lecturer, reviewer, and critic. He was suspicious of the label of "professional philosopher," but was still active in the French intellectual scene where he knew and frequently met other luminaries of the time such as Jacques Maritain, Jean Paul Sartre, Paul Ricoeur, Charles Du Bos, and Jean Wahl. In his later career, Marcel traveled extensively in Europe and in the United States, and became more widely known. He delivered the prestigious Gifford lectures at the University of Aberdeen in 1949–50; published in two volumes as *Le mystère de l'être* (*The Mystery of Being*, two vols., 1951), they are the most systematic, detailed presentation of his thought. Marcel also delivered the William James lectures at Harvard in 1951, using the occasion to elaborate on the important connection between theater and philosophy. These lectures were later published as *The Existential Background of Human Dignity* (1963). His other main works are: *Homo Viator*: *Prolégomenes à une métaphysique de l'espérance* (*Homo Viator: Introduction to a Metaphysic of Hope*, 1944); *De refus à l'invocation* (*Creative Fidelity*, 1940), and *Les Hommes contre l'humain* (*Man against Mass Society*, 1951). Marcel was also a playwright, and wrote more than a dozen plays, many of which illustrate in concrete form various themes from his philosophy. He died in 1973.

Marcel's thought can be accurately described as "existentialist" in the sense that he accepts that philosophy begins with concrete human experience; he gives concrete human experience an ontological priority when doing philosophy over a purely reflective approach that emphasizes abstract logical arguments and conceptual analysis of philosophical questions, usually divorced from the concrete lived experience of the human person. However, he repudiated the terms "existentialist" and "existentialism" as descriptions of his thought mainly because these terms had a rather negative connotation during the 1940s due to their association (through Jean-Paul Sartre, 1905–1980) with an atheistic, pessimistic worldview, and because he didn't think philosophy could ever become an "ism" without betraying itself.

Marcel is also a critic of the Cartesian approach to philosophy that has developed out of the thought of Descartes, especially the traditional epistemological problems which Cartesianism has given rise to (and with which some branches of contemporary philosophy have become obsessed), like, for example, the problem of skepticism. His critique of the Cartesian approach is essentially a critique of that account of the nature of the self upon which the traditional epistemological enterprise is based. Marcel believes that the Cartesian view of the self is not a presentation of how the self actually is. Descartes focused too much on the analysis of clear and distinct ideas, and overlooked the fact that our first contact with the world is just that – contact, without any mediation from clear and distinct ideas (i.e., abstractions), or clear representations. Marcel holds that it is our fundamental situation in the world which defines our "ideas," and any analysis or description of them must involve a reference to a human body, and its place or "situation" in existence. Descartes missed this understanding of the human subject, and adopted what Marcel calls a "spectator view" of the self; Descartes also mistakenly made conceptual knowledge the paradigm of knowledge.

Marcel believes, however, that conceptual knowledge is unable to give an adequate account of what he calls the "being-in-a-situation," or what I call the "situated involvement," of the subject in his or her world. According to Marcel, the subject is fundamentally an embodied being-in-a-situation, and is not solely a thinking or knowing subject. This is because the subject is always located in a specific context by virtue of his or her particular embodied situation in the world. This embodied situation is defined by the subject's particular spatial and temporal location, general and personal history, cultural and economic context, and so forth. This is a realm where the subject's experiences take place at the level of existential contact, and not at the level of abstraction. The basic level of being-in-a-situation, according to Marcel, is not fully accessible to conceptual or theoretical thinking, nor are what are sometimes called the higher levels of being of moral experience, human relationships, or the subject's relationship with God. This point is significant because one of the abuses of modern thought is its tendency to try to objectify all human experience in concepts, and failing this, to judge that any experience which cannot be so objectified is not a worthy subject for philosophical analysis. Marcel wishes to challenge and correct this contemporary dogma and in so doing to preserve and defend the integrity and dignity of the human person.

Marcel offers some penetrating insights on the nature of reflection. Reflection may be understood as a form of attention to our pre-reflective lived experiences, which are habitual and ontologically primary. He makes an important distinction between primary and secondary reflection. Primary reflection is ordinary, everyday reflection, which employs conceptual generalizations, abstractions, and an appeal to what is universal and verifiable. This kind of thinking seeks demonstrable connections and is the kind of reflection found in the sciences, mathematics, and "theoretical thinking" of any kind, including philosophy itself. It involves a "standing back" from, or abstraction from, our fundamental involvement with things, and engages in an inquiry which proceeds by means of disinterested concepts, which have shareable, public, and, therefore, universal content.

Marcel famously points out that this type of reflection typically deals with problems of various kinds. A "problem," as Marcel understands the term, is a project which requires a solution that is available for everybody, such, as for example, finding out why an electrical circuit will not operate. A problem presupposes a community of inquiry in which the problem can be (publicly) formulated, and hopefully solved. But features of experience can only be presented as "problems" for the mind if the individual first abstracts from the "situated involvement" which defines the lived experience of the inquirer, and these features can only be maintained and discussed as problems if everyone involved in their appraisal does likewise. Therefore, primary reflection is the means by which it is possible for the community of human beings to collectively formulate and discuss problems, and to attempt to arrive at solutions to them. Characterized in this way, primary reflection is obviously a very important feature of the ontological structure of human beings, a fact that Marcel does not wish to deny. In addition, primary reflection is also the level of objective knowledge. This is because the concepts employed at the theoretical level are objective in two key senses. First, they represent essential features of the objects of experience (at an abstract level) as they really are in the objects, and second, these essential features are also objective in the key sense that they are understood by everyone in the same way.

Marcel contrasts the realm of problems with the realm of mystery, which is a realm where the distinction between subject and object breaks down. The most basic level of human existence, being-in-a-situation, or situated involvement, is the level at which the subject is immersed in a context, a level where the subject does not experience "objects" (in the sense that would be typical of primary reflection, or problematical thinking). This realm of human existence is best described as "mysterious," from the philosophical point of view, because it cannot be fully captured and presented in ordinary conceptual knowledge. It is even difficult to reveal or evoke in phenomenological descriptions. It is not an unknowable realm, but a realm which is beyond conceptual knowledge, and which must be experienced to some extent to be truly known. Some of the "mysteries" of Being, according to Marcel, are our experience of our own embodiment, the unity of body and mind, the nature of sensation, and the higher levels of being: the "concrete approaches" of love, hope, fidelity, and faith. These experiences are all mysterious because they intimately and essentially involve the questioner in such a way that the meaning of the experience cannot be fully conveyed by means of abstract conceptual thinking, i.e., by cutting the individual subject off from the experience.

Marcel introduces the notion of secondary reflection to show us how to go beyond the realm of primary reflection. Secondary reflection is best understood as both the act of critical reflection on primary reflection, and the process of recovery of the "mysteries of being." Therefore, secondary reflection is best characterized as beginning with an act of critical reflection (a "second" reflection) on ordinary conceptual thinking (primary reflection). This "second" or critical reflection enables the philosopher to discover that the categories of primary reflection are not adequate to provide a true account of the nature of the self, or the self's most profound experiences. Here secondary reflection involves ordinary reflection, but with the crucial difference that, unlike ordinary reflection, it is a critical reflection directed at the nature of thought itself. The act of secondary reflection then culminates in a realization, or discovery, of the realm of mystery, and motivates human actions appropriate to this realm. This discovery is a kind of intuitive grasp or experiential awareness of various experiences which are non-conceptual, and which conceptual knowledge can never fully express.

This new dimension to which secondary reflection allows us access is what Marcel often refers to as the realm of being, or of the unity of experience. This realm is also the guide (the "intuition") of reflective thought. It also provides an insight into the realm of value. Our experience of the value-laden nature of being also gives us an insight into the transcendent nature of human existence. The idea here is that there is a transcendent aspect to human existence because it is already endowed with value, which no individual brought to it, or created, but which we recognize, and which will exist after we are gone. This view of transcendence does not emphasize transcendence understood in the sense of being the result of an objective demonstration (though Marcel does not deny this sense), but rather in the sense that it is something we can recognize in our own experience. In this sense, Marcel suggests that perhaps the experience of transcendence should not be primarily understood as something that comes from outside us, although it clearly has an independence from any one individual. But transcendence can also be understood as a kind of reaching out of myself toward the intersubjective nature of existence, a reaching out which is an essential part of human existence, and without which we are not fulfilled. For Marcel, this experience of transcendence can eventually lead to the affirmation of God, and indeed he argues that it requires the existence of God for its ultimate justification, whether a particular individual recognizes this or acknowledges it.

This brings us to Marcel's notion of *disponibilité*, usually translated as "availability" in English. The notion of availability can be seen as a more practical statement of how our actual behavior toward other human beings is to be conducted. The notion of disponibilité is meant to convey the idea of a kind of "spiritual availability" which we should adopt toward other human beings. It is the idea that we should approach other human beings with an openness and humility; we should not be aloof or egocentric, or obsessed with our own affairs. Unavailability (*indisponibilité*), on the other hand, is a hardening of the categories in accordance with which we conceive and evaluate the world. Modern society, with its emphasis on primary reflection, and scientism, has smothered disponibilité, ushering in a new kind of alienation. Marcel believes we need a reawakening of all that is spiritual in humanity, including our sense of the transcendent, both in inter-personal relationships and in our relationship with God.

Another more obvious way to understand Marcel's notion of disponibilité is in terms of Martin Buber's distinction between I-It and I-Thou relations, an analysis of human relations which Marcel strongly endorses. The I-Thou relation is spoken with one's whole being, according to Buber; it involves a dialogue with the other, in which one is a participant and not merely a spectator. Such relations involve risk and sacrifice, they are the basis of true freedom, and they lead to the fulfillment of the human person. One can refuse these relations as we said earlier, and the modern world is becoming increasingly dominated by I-It relationships, yet the phenomenological analysis of I-Thou relations accurately captures the inexpressible depth of human relationships.

This world of disponibilité is the complete opposite to the world of I-It, of primary reflection, which, we have seen, is the world of abstraction, manipulation, possession, a world of "having" which seeks solutions to universal, public problems of different kinds. Marcel argues that the problem with modern attitudes is that they are more and more dominated by primary reflection; this is even true of our attitude toward the human subject, which can become just another object, which needs to be analyzed in the way all objects are analyzed. Marcel sometimes describes the modern world as a "broken world" (*le monde cassé*) to reflect the fact that we are losing the realm of being and availability, upon which authentic human relationships and the spirit of transcendence are founded.

This is just a brief sketch of some of Marcel's main ideas. His work is full of remarkable and thoughtful insights that speak to many of our concerns today. I invite readers to experience the profundity and richness of his thinking for themselves.

I wish to acknowledge a number of people who helped me while I worked on this book. Henri Marcel, who provided me with new photographs of his grandfather, one of which is used on the cover, was always supportive of the project. I also owe a depth of gratitude to Bruce Fingerhut, and his staff at St. Augustine's Press, for their advice, support and hard work. Acknowledgements are also due to Rockhurst University which provided grant support for work on the book. I also gratefully acknowledge permissions to reprint from Marcel's works from Northwestern University Press, Kensington Books, Paulist Press and St. Augustine's Press. And, as always, thanks to my family for their unfailing support.

Brendan Sweetman
Kansas City, Summer 2010

Chapter 1

The Nature of Philosophy

Marcel explains in these selections that he does not conceive of philosophy as a system of propositions, and notes that his own method in philosophy has always been to a significant extent non-systematic and non-objective. This approach facilitates a more accurate insight into the non-transparent nature of human experience, and allows us to appreciate that the scientific approach to reality, which he illustrates by means of several examples, should not be regarded by philosophers as the paradigm of knowledge. Whereas the scientific approach seeks universal, demonstrable solutions that are available to everybody, philosophical inquiry is the exact opposite. It is a type of inquiry that requires the existential involvement of the person engaged in the task of doing philosophy; that is, the philosopher must be involved or engaged in some way in the philosophical question, and cannot be detached in the way a chemist, for example, can be detached from the results of his or her research.

Marcel's style of philosophizing expects readers to think along with him, to clarify his insights in relation to their own experiences. The main aim of any philosophical inquiry is the attempt to discover the most basic truths about the human condition. Marcel wishes to reveal the necessary connections which constitute the meaning of a particular human subject's experiences in his or her concrete embodied situation in existence. (Necessary connections refer to those parts of our experience, including our conceptual knowledge, that must go together in some way in order to understand the meanings present in knowledge and experience.) However, Marcel's approach does not avoid the pure, detached objectivity sought in science only to end up in subjectivism; instead, like art, philosophical inquiry seeks objective truths about the human condition that are open to minds of a certain sort, but not necessarily to everyone. Truth in philosophy is therefore not a "thing," and philosophy does not aim at "practical results," but tries to allow human experience to reflect upon itself in order to reveal its own essential ("objective") structures. The last paragraph notes the connection between philosophy and Christianity.

* * *

The Nature of Philosophy

. . . philosophy, like art or poetry, rests on a foundation of personal involvement, or to use a more profoundly meaningful expression, it has its source in a vocation, where the word "vocation" is taken with all its etymological significance. I think that philosophy, regarded in its essential finality, has to be considered as a personal response to a call. [TWB, p. 3]

* * *

When I called these lectures a search for, or an investigation into, the essence of spiritual reality, I was not choosing words at random. From my point of view such a term as search or investigation – some term implying the notion of a quest – is the most adequate description that can be applied to the essential direction of philosophy. Philosophy will always, to my way of thinking, be an aid to discovery rather than a matter of strict demonstration. And, if pressed, I would expand that; I think the philosopher who first discovers certain truths and then sets out to expound them in their dialectical or systematic interconnections always runs the risk of profoundly altering the nature of the truths he has discovered.

Furthermore, I will not disguise from you the fact that when I had been nominated by the University of Aberdeen to deliver the Gifford Lectures in 1949 and 1950, my first reaction was a feeling of intense inner disturbance. The honor that was being done to me faced me with a serious personal problem. Was I not, in fact, being asked to do something which it had been my constant determination not to do: namely, to present in a systematic form material which, I repeat, has always remained for me at the stage of a quest? . . .

. . . At the same time, it was clear to me that in answering this call I must continue to respect the specific character of what has always been my own line of development. And, of course, those who made this offer [of presenting the lectures] to me would have that line of development in view. Nobody who had any direct knowledge of my writings would dream of expecting from me an exposition in the deductive manner, the logical linking together of a body of essential propositions.

. . . Well, looking at the matter in my own way, I must ask whether, in the realm of philosophy, we can really talk about results? Is not all such talk based on a misunderstanding of the specific character of a philosophical investigation, as such? The question raised here at least obliges us to come to much closer grips with the very notion of a result.

Let us take the case of a chemist who has invented and set going some process for obtaining or extracting a substance which, before his time, could only be got hold of in a much more costly and complicated fashion. It is obvious, in this case, that the result of the invention will have a sort of separate existence, or, at all events, that we shall be quite within our rights in treating it as if it had. If I need the substance – let us say it is some pharmaceutical product – I will go to the shop, and I will not need to know that it is thanks to the invention of the chemist in question that I am able to procure it easily. In my purely practical role as customer and consumer, I may have no occasion even to learn that there has been such an invention unless for some out-of-the-way reason; let us say, because a factory has been destroyed and the invention has temporarily ceased to be put into operation. The pharmacist may then tell me that the product is out of stock, or is not to be had at its usual price and quality, but let us get it quite clear that in the ordinary run of affairs the existence of this chemical process will be known only to specialists or to those who are moving in the direction of specialization. Here we have a very simple example indeed of what sort of life a result may lead, cut apart from the methods by which it was achieved. And one could go on to mention many other examples; it is not necessary that a result should always embody itself, as in the instance I have given, as a material commodity. Think of some astronomical forecast, say of a coming eclipse. We welcome that, we make it our own, without bothering ourselves much about the extremely complicated calculations on which it is founded, and knowing quite well that our own mathematical equipment is not sufficient to allow us to do these sums over again in our own heads.

One might note here, in passing, that in our modern world, because of its extreme technical complication, we are, in fact, condemned to take for granted a great many results achieved through long research and laborious calculations, research and calculations of which the details are bound to escape us.

One might postulate it as a principle, on the other hand, that in an investigation of the type on which we are now engaged, a philosophical investigation, there can be no place at all for results of this sort. Let us expand that: between a philosophical investigation and its final outcome, there exists a link which cannot be broken without the summing up itself immediately losing all reality. And of course we must also ask ourselves here just what we mean, in this context, by *reality*.

We can come to the same conclusions starting from the other end. We can attempt to elucidate the notion of philosophical investigation directly. Where a technician, like the chemist, starts off with some very general notion, a notion given in advance of what he is looking for, what is peculiar to a philosophical investigation is that the man who undertakes it cannot possess anything equivalent to that notion given in advance of what he is looking for. It would not, perhaps, be imprecise to say that he starts off at random; I am taking care not to forget that this has been sometimes the case with scientists themselves, but a scientific result achieved, so to say, by a happy accident acquires a kind of purpose when it is viewed retrospectively; it looks as if it had tended towards some strictly specific aim. As we go on we shall gradually see more and more clearly that this can never be the case with philosophic investigation.

On the other hand, when we think of it, we realize that our mental image of the technician – of the scientist, too, for at this level the distinction between the two of them reaches vanishing point – is that of a man perpetually carrying out operations, in his own mind or with physical objects, which anybody could carry out in his place. The sequence of these operations, for that reason, can be schematized in universal terms. I am abstracting here from the mental gropings which are inseparable, in the individual scientist's history, from all periods of discovery. These gropings are like the useless roundabout routes taken by a raw tourist in a country with which he has not yet made himself familiar. Both are destined to be dropped and forgotten, for good and all, once the traveler knows the lie of the land.

The greatness and the limitation of scientific discovery consist precisely in the fact that it is bound by its nature to be lost in anonymity. Once a result has been achieved, it is bound to appear, if not a matter of chance, at least a matter of contingence, that it should have been this man and not that man who discovered such and such a process. This retrospective view of the matter is probably in some degree an illusion, but the illusion is itself inseparable from the general pattern of scientific research. From the point of view of technical progress, there is no point in considering the concrete conditions in which some discovery was actually able to be made, the personal, the perhaps tragic background from which the discovery, as such, detaches itself; from the strictly technical point of view all that background is, obviously and inevitably, something to be abstracted from.

But this is not and cannot be true in the same way for the kind of investigation that will be presented in the course of these lectures; and it is essential to see exactly why not. How can we start out on a search without having somehow anticipated what we are searching for? Here, again, it is necessary to make certain distinctions. The notion given in advance, the scientist's or technician's notion, which in a philosophical investigation we must exclude, has to do, in fact, with a certain way of acting: the problem is how to set about it so that some mode of action which is at the moment impracticable, or at least can only be carried out in unsatisfactory and precarious conditions, should become practicable according to certain pre-established standards of practicability (standards of simplicity, of economy, and so on). Let us add, in addition, as a development of what has previously been said, that this mode of action should be of a sort that can be carried out by anybody, at least by anybody within a certain determinable set of conditions, anybody, for instance, equipped with certain indispensable tools.

It is probably not sufficient for my purpose merely to say that, where a metaphysical investigation is being undertaken, a result of this sort, the arrival at a practicable mode of action within certain determinable conditions, cannot be calculated on in advance, and that in fact the very idea of a metaphysical investigation necessarily excludes the possibility of this kind of practical result. For I might also add that the inaptitude of the run of men for metaphysics, particularly in our own period, is certainly bound up with the fact that they find it impossible to conceive of a purpose which lies outside the order of the practical, which cannot be translated into the language of action. . . .

. . . The really important question that is raised may be framed in the following terms: is there not a risk of the investigation that is being undertaken here reducing itself to an account of the succession of stages by which I, I as this particular person, Gabriel Marcel, attempt, starting off from some state of being which implies a certain suffering, to reach another state of being which not only does not imply suffering but may be accompanied by a certain joy? But what guarantee can I have that this personal progress of mine has anything more than a subjective value? . . .

. . . Let us say, to put it very roughly, that the dilemma in which this question leaves us – that of choice between the actual individual man, delivered over to his own states of being and incapable of transcending them, and a kind of generalized thinking as such, what the Germans call

Denken uberhaupt, which would be operative in a sort of Absolute and so claim universal validity for its operations – let us say that this dilemma is a false one, and must be rejected. Between these two antithetic terms, we must intercalate an intermediary type of thinking, which is precisely the type of thinking that the lecture following this will illustrate. The point should at once be made here that, even outside the limits of philosophy properly so called, there are incontestable examples of this type of thinking. We have only to think, for instance, of what we describe, rather vaguely indeed, as the understanding of works of art; it would be better no doubt, in this connection, to talk of their appreciation – so long as we eliminate from that word its root reference to a *pretium*, a market price. It would be an illusion and even an absurdity to suppose that the *Missa Solemnis* or some great work of pictorial art is meant for just anybody who comes along; on the contrary, we must in honest sincerity accept the fact that there are plenty of people whose attention is not arrested, and who have nothing communicated to them, by such works. It is none the less certain that when a genuine emotion is felt at the impact of a work of art it infinitely transcends the limits of what we call the individual consciousness. . . .

. . . The task of philosophy, to my mind, consists precisely in this sort of reciprocal clarification of two unknowns, and it may well be that, in order to pose the true questions, it is actually necessary to have an intuition, in advance, about what the true answers might be. It might be said that the true questions are those which point, not to anything resembling the solution of an enigma, but rather to a line of direction along which we must move. As we move along the line, we get more and more chances of being visited by a sort of spiritual illumination; for we shall have to acknowledge that Truth can be considered only in this way, as a spirit, as a light. [MBI, pp. 1–13]

*   *   *

Before pressing further forward, I feel it necessary to go back a little, to consider certain objections that will have undoubtedly occurred to many of my listeners.

I assert that an investigation of the sort in which we are engaged, an investigation of an eminently theoretical kind, can appeal only to minds of a certain sort, to minds that have already a special bias. Is there not something strange and almost shocking in such an assertion? Does it not imply a perversion of the very notion of truth? The ordinary idea of truth, the normal idea of truth, surely involves a universal reference – what is true, that is to say, is true for anybody and everybody. Are we not risking a great deal in wrenching apart, in this way, the two notions of *the true* and the *universally valid*? Or more exactly, in making this distinction, are we not substituting for the notion of truth some other notion – some value which may have its place in the practical, the moral, or the aesthetic order, but for which truth is not the proper term?. . . What the objection implies, in fact, is that we know in advance, and perhaps even know in a quite schematic fashion, what the relation between the self and the truth it recognizes must be.

In the last two or three centuries, and indeed since much more remote periods, there has been a great deal of critical reflection on the subject of truth. Nevertheless, there is every reason to suppose that, in our everyday thinking, we remain dominated by an image of truth as something extracted – extracted, or smelted out, exactly as a pure metal is extracted from a mixed ore. It seems obvious to us that there are universally effective smelting processes: or, more fundamentally, that there are established, legitimate ways of arriving at truth; and we have a confused feeling that the man who steps aside from these ways, or even from the idea of these ways, is in danger of losing himself in a sort of no man's land where the difference between truth and error – even between reality and dream – tends to vanish away. It is, however, this very image of truth as something smelted out that we must encounter critically if we want to grasp clearly the gross error on which it rests. What we must above all reject is the idea that we are forced to make a choice between a genuine truth (so to call it) which has been extracted, and a false, a lying truth which has been fabricated. Both horns of this dilemma, it should be noted, are metaphorically modeled on physical processes; and there is, on the face of it, every reason to suppose that the subtle labor involved in the search for truth cannot ever be properly assimilated to such physical manipulations of physical objects. But truth is not a *thing;* whatever definition we may in the end be induced to give to the notion of truth, we can affirm even now that truth is not a physical object, that the search for truth is not a physical process, that no generalizations that apply to physical objects and processes can apply also to truth. . . .

. . . On the one hand, everything that can be properly called technique is comparable to a kind of manipulation, if not always necessarily of physical objects, at least of mental elements (mathematical symbols would be an example) comparable in some respects to physical objects; and I suggest on the other hand that the validity for anybody and everybody, which has been claimed for truth, is certainly deeply implied (though even here, subject to certain provisos) in the very notion of technique, as we have conceived that notion here. Subject to certain provisos, I say, since every technical manipulation, even the simplest, implies the possession by the manipulator of certain minimal aptitudes, without which it is not practicable. There is a story, for instance, that I often tell, of how I had to pass an examination in physics which included, as a practical test, an experiment to determine one of the simpler electrical formulae – I forget which now, let us say the laws of electrolysis – and I found myself quite incapable of joining up the wires properly, so no current came through. All I could do was write on my paper, "I cannot join up my wires, so there is no current; if there were a current, it would produce such and such a phenomenon, and I would deduce. . . ." My own clumsiness appeared to me, and it must have appeared to the examiner, as a purely contingent fact. It remains true *in principle* that anybody and everybody can join up the wires, enable the current to pass through, and so on.

Conversely, we must say that the further the intelligence passes beyond the limits of a purely technical activity, the less the reference to the "no matter whom," the "anybody at all," is applicable; and that in the extreme case there will be no sense at all in saying that such and such a task of lofty reflection could have been carried out by anybody whatsoever. One might even say, as I indicated in my first chapter, that the philosopher's task involves not only unusual mental aptitudes but an unusual sense of inner urgent need; and as I have already suggested, towards the end of that chapter, we shall have to face the fact that in such a world as we live in urgent inner needs of this type are almost systematically misunderstood, are even deliberately discredited. [MBI, pp. 18–21]

*   *   *

The kind of inquiry I have in mind will be governed by an obligation which is not easy to formulate; it is not sufficient to say that it is an avowal of fidelity to experience; an examination of philosophical empiricism shows the extent to which the term "experience" is vague and ambiguous. Philosophy provides the means for experience to become aware of itself, to apprehend itself – but at what level of experience? And how can such a hierarchy be established or defined? My only comment here is that we must distinguish not only degrees of clarification but degrees of intimacy with oneself and with one's surroundings – with the universe itself.

This inquiry must be based on a certitude which is not rational or logical but existential; if existence is not at the beginning it is nowhere, for I do not believe that any transition can be made to existence which is not cheating or deception. [CF, p. 15]

* * *

What does it mean to philosophize concretely? This question does not at all imply a return to empiricism. . . . We are nearer to the truth if we say that it is to philosophize *hic et nunc*. I want to clarify what I mean by this, but I can only do so in a polemical manner, i.e., by opposing a certain official philosophy or pseudo-philosophy. . . .

First, with respect to the history of philosophy. Of course, a philosopher should "know" the history of philosophy, but to my mind he should know it more or less in the sense in which a composer knows harmony; that is, possessing the tools of harmony without ever becoming their slave. From the moment he is their slave, he is no longer a creator or an artist. Similarly, the philosopher who has surrendered to the history of philosophy is, to that extent, not a philosopher. . . .

Whoever philosophizes *hic et nunc* is, it may be said, a prey of reality; he will never become completely accustomed to the fact of existing; existence is inseparable from a certain astonishment. . . .

Personally, I am inclined to deny that any work is philosophical if we cannot discern in it what may be called the sting of reality. . . .

It may be said in this respect that no concrete philosophy is possible without a constantly renewed yet creative tension between the I and those depths of our being in and by which we are; nor without the most stringent and rigorous reflection, directed on our most intensely lived experience. . . .

. . . a concrete philosophy cannot fail to be magnetically attracted to the data of Christianity, perhaps without knowing it. And I do not think that this fact should shock anyone. For the Christian, there is an essential agreement between Christianity and human nature. Hence the more deeply one penetrates into human nature, the more one finds oneself situated on the axes of the great truths of Christianity. An objection will be raised: You affirm this as a Christian, not as a philosopher. Here, I can only repeat what I said at the beginning: the philosopher who compels himself to think only as a philosopher places himself on the hither side of experience in an infrahuman realm; but philosophy implies an exaltation of experience, not a castration of it. [CF, pp. 61–80]

Chapter 2

On Epistemology and the Nature of Knowledge

Marcel's "On the Ontological Mystery" is one of the clearest, most sequential presentations of his main ideas to be found anywhere in his work, which makes it an especially useful essay for readers. It serves as a good introduction to the heart of his phenomenological ontology, in which he is concerned with ontological questions concerning the kind of beings we are, and how we come to gain knowledge and understanding. The essay is also a good illustration of the experiential dimension of Marcel's thought, and provides an overview of his central themes: being, reflection (both primary and secondary), problem and mystery, fidelity, hope, presence, spiritual availability, and the relationship between his philosophy and Christianity.

Marcel opens the essay by noting that human beings today are increasingly defined by their functions: vital, social and psychological. Our world is dominated by problems that require technical solutions, and that leave no room for mystery. This situation invites an inner despair because the ontological need for being is suppressed. While the notion of being is hard to define, he suggests that it is primarily an experience, one that resists an exhaustive conceptual description; it also refers to the life of the spirit, a life that much of modern thought is usually in denial about. From the philosophical point of view, being is a realm where the real human self is revealed through careful phenomenological descriptions, a realm to which secondary reflection allows us access. Being is not deduced from an analysis of theoretical thinking but is actually the guide (the "intuition") of reflective thought. This is the realm of mystery where the distinction between subject and object breaks down. Marcel illustrates with several examples: the union of body and soul, the experience of evil (as distinct from a consideration of evil as an abstract problem), inter-personal relations (especially the experience of love), experiences of fidelity, religious experiences, and experiences requiring ethical responses to human beings and events. Although difficult to describe, Marcel argues that this realm of being is objectively real, and can be revealed to some extent in conceptual knowledge, especially through philosophy, a task he is attempting in this essay. The problem is that one cannot dissociate the idea of being from the certainty that pertains to it. Indeed, the idea is an assurance of itself, a view that is the antithesis of the Cartesian approach, which is founded on the idea that being and thought are initially separate (and so the problem is how to get them back together).

Marcel offers some reflections on "recollection," on secondary reflection, which he describes as a process of reflection that helps us to recover the experiences appropriate to the realm of being. Secondary reflection is best understood as both the act of critical reflection on primary reflection, and the process of recovery of the "mysteries of being." He then turns back to the topic of despair, which is a possible, but misguided, response to the human condition. The counter-experience to despair is the experience of hope – an experience of trust or confidence in human life, and its meaning and value. This form of hope is grounded, not in external events, but in the depths of what I am as a human being; it is an ontological experience that ultimately points in a transcendental direction.

These experiences make sense at the level of mystery, but sometimes not at the level of problems. Marcel offers a similar analysis of the experience of fidelity, and introduces the illuminating notion of presence. This leads him to the idea of "disponibilité," or "spiritual availability," the idea that we should approach other human beings with openness and humility; and not with selfishness or egotism. Along the way, he considers various objections, and concludes with a very revealing discussion of the relationship between his philosophy and Christianity. (I have added subject headings throughout "On the Ontological Mystery" as a way of introducing the various themes of the essay.)

In Part 2 of this chapter, we come to Marcel's existentialist critique of Cartesianism, which is essentially a critique of that account of the self upon which the whole of traditional epistemology is based, a conception of the self that has been extremely influential in modern and contemporary philosophy. It is the foundation for the obsession with the problem of skepticism in modern analytical philosophy, along with the search for objectively demonstrable knowledge, as well as being the motivation for various relativistic and anti-realist alternatives (e.g., in postmodernism). The problem of skepticism, for Marcel, is generated by artificially divorcing the knowing subject from the world of external objects. At the level of ordinary primary reflection, the problems of the existence of external objects, of the existence of the body, and of the relationship of these objects to the mind, do not arise. In the traditional view of the self (the "universal" ego), the personal experience of the subject is removed in the act of abstraction, so that all we are left with is isolated, sharable, and, therefore, disinterested concepts, i.e., the world of primary reflection. But it is not possible to motivate any kind of global skepticism from this vantage point.

In Part 3, Marcel argues that the self is fundamentally an embodied subject, which means that my embodiment is partly constitutive of the kinds of experiences I have, experiences which make me the person I am. Reflection upon the notion of ownership, Marcel suggests, reveals that I cannot regard my body as my possession; the body is, rather, a condition of possessing something, and so cannot itself be possessed. This means that the nature of the relationship of the self to the body cannot be fully captured in objective thought. Marcel describes this relationship as "mysterious," not because it is unknowable, but because, although it can be known by the subject, it nevertheless cannot be fully articulated in conceptual analysis. In addition, contrary to one of the key steps in Descartes' formulation of the problem of skepticism, it is not logically possible for me to regard the existence of my own body as the occasion for a problem, i.e., as a subject for a disinterested inquiry, because my body involves me, and as soon as I regard it as a problem, I no longer regard it as "my" body.

Marcel next (in Part 4) turns to primary and secondary reflection, pointing out that primary reflection tends to dissolve the unity of experience by abstracting from it and looking at various features of it as problems to be solved, which is an important part of reflection, but not the whole, nor indeed the main, part. The main form of reflection, secondary reflection, involves the attempt to recover the unity of experience. He links these notions to the notion of embodiment, which is the foundation of the initial unity because it places us in a realm of experiences, which reflection then breaks apart; a realm, further, that also confirms the assurance of our own existence in the world. Marcel also briefly addresses the problem of how to conceptualize the notion of secondary reflection without debasing it. He continues these themes in Part 5 on problem and mystery, and emphasizes again the point that a "mystery" does not refer to a gap in our knowledge.

Marcel has been striving in these selections to reach a vantage point from which his main themes can be best understood, and from where he can be seen as offering a unified account of the human condition. This attempt inevitably brings him to the notion of being in Part 6, where he brings together a number of important themes: that it is impossible not to adopt the realist solution to the problem of being; the relation between thought and being (and the relevance of the principle of identity for ordinary logical reasoning); how various philosophical approaches can either deny or affirm, but cannot avoid, being; how the realm of being provides a powerful illustration of the difference between a mystery and a problem; how the realm of being points us in a transcendental direction; and the important relationship between being and value.

*   *   *

1. On the Ontological Mystery

The title of this essay is likely to annoy the philosopher as much as to startle the layman, since philosophers are inclined to leave mystery either to the theologians or else to the vulgarizers, whether of mysticism or of occultism, such as Maeterlinck. Moreover, the term *ontological*, which has only the vaguest meaning for the layman, has become discredited in the eyes of Idealist philosophers; while the term *mystery* is reserved by those thinkers who are imbued with the ideas of Scholasticism for the revealed mysteries of religion.

Thus my terminology is clearly open to criticism from all sides. But I can find no other which is adequate to the body of ideas which I intend to put forward and on which my whole outlook is based. Readers of my *Journal métaphysique* will see that they represent the term of the whole spiritual and philosophical evolution which I have described in that book.

Rather than to begin with abstract definitions and dialectical arguments which may be discouraging at the outset, I should like to start with a sort of global and intuitive characterization of the man in whom the sense of the ontological – the sense of being – is lacking, or, to speak more correctly, of the man who has lost the awareness of this sense. Generally speaking, modern man is in this condition; if ontological demands worry him at all, it is only dully, as an obscure impulse. Indeed I wonder if a psychoanalytical method, deeper and more discerning than any that has been evolved until now, would not reveal the morbid effects of the repression of this sense and of the ignoring of this need.

Human Beings Defined by Their Functions

The characteristic feature of our age seems to me to be what might be called the misplacement of the idea of function, taking function in its current sense which includes both the vital and the social functions.

The individual tends to appear both to himself and to others as an agglomeration of functions. As a result of deep historical causes, which can as yet be understood only in part, he has been led to see himself more and more as a mere assemblage of functions, the hierarchical interrelation of which seems to him questionable or at least subject to conflicting interpretations.

To take the vital functions first. It is hardly necessary to point out the role which historical materialism on the one hand, and Freudian doctrines on the other, have played in restricting the concept of man.

Then there are the social functions – those of the consumer, the producer, the citizen, etc.

Between these two there is, in theory, room for the psychological functions as well; but it is easy to see how these will tend to be interpreted in relation either to the social or the vital functions, so that their independence will be threatened and their specific character put in doubt. In this sense, Comte, served by his total incomprehension of psychical reality, displayed an almost prophetic instinct when he excluded psychology from his classification of sciences.

So far we are still dealing only with abstractions, but nothing is easier than to find concrete illustrations in this field.

Traveling on the Underground, I often wonder with a kind of dread what can be the inward reality of the life of this or that man employed on the railway – the man who opens the doors, for instance, or the one who punches the tickets. Surely everything both within him and outside him conspires to identify this man with his functions – meaning not only with his functions as worker, as trade union member or as voter, but with his vital functions as well. The rather horrible expression "time table" perfectly describes his life. So many hours for each function. Sleep too is a function which must be discharged so that the other functions may be exercised in their turn. The same with pleasure, with relaxation; it is logical that the weekly allowance of recreation should be determined by an expert on hygiene; recreation is a psycho-organic function which must not be neglected any more than, for instance, the function of sex. We need go no further; this sketch is sufficient to suggest the emergence of a kind of vital schedule; the details will vary with the country, the climate, the profession, etc., but what matters is that there is a schedule.

It is true that certain disorderly elements – sickness, accidents of every sort – will break in on the smooth working of the system. It is therefore natural that the individual should be overhauled at regular intervals like a watch (this is often done in America). The hospital plays the part of the inspection bench or the repair shop. And it is from this same standpoint of function that such essential problems as birth control will be examined.

As for death, it becomes, objectively and functionally, the scrapping of what has ceased to be of use and must be written off as a total loss.

I need hardly insist on the stifling impression of sadness produced by this fictionalized world. It is sufficient to recall the dreary image of the retired official, or those urban Sundays when the passers-by look like people who have retired from life. In such a world, there is something mocking and sinister even in the tolerance awarded to the man who has retired from his work.

But besides the sadness felt by the onlooker, there is the dull, intolerable unease of the actor himself who is reduced to living as though he were in fact submerged by his functions. This uneasiness is enough to show that there is in all this some appalling mistake, some ghastly misinterpretation, implanted in defenseless minds by an increasingly inhuman social order and an equally inhuman philosophy (for if the philosophy has prepared the way for the order, the order has also shaped the philosophy).

The Ontological Need for Being

I have written on another occasion that, provided it is taken in its metaphysical and not its physical sense, the distinction between the *full* and the *empty* seems to me more fundamental than that between the *one* and the *many*. This is particularly applicable to the case in point. Life in a world centered on function is liable to despair because in reality this world is *empty*, it rings hollow; and if it resists this temptation it is only to the extent that there come into play from within it and in its favor certain hidden forces which are beyond its power to conceive or to recognize.

It should be noted that this world is, on the one hand, riddled with problems and, on the other, determined to allow no room for mystery. I shall come back to this distinction between problem and mystery which I believe to be fundamental. For the moment I shall only point out that to eliminate or to try to eliminate mystery is (in this functionalist world) to bring into play in the face of events which break in on the course of existence – such as birth, love and death – that psychological and pseudo-scientific category of the "purely natural" which deserves a study to itself. In reality, this is nothing more than the remains of a degraded rationalism from whose standpoint cause explains effect and accounts for it exhaustively. There exists in such a world, nevertheless, an infinity of problems, since the causes are not known to us in detail and thus leave room for unlimited research. And in addition to these theoretical puzzles there are innumerable technical problems, bound up with the difficulty of knowing how the various functions, once they have been inventoried and labeled, can be made to work together without doing one another harm. These theoretical and technical questions are interdependent, for the theoretical problems arise out of the different techniques while the technical problems can not be solved without a measure of pre-established theoretical knowledge.

In such a world the ontological need, the need of being, is exhausted in exact proportion to the breaking up of personality on the one hand and, on the other, to the triumph of the category of the "purely natural" and the consequent atrophy of the faculty of *wonder*.

But to come at last to the ontological need itself: can we not approach it directly and attempt to define it? In reality this can only be done to a limited extent. For reasons which I shall develop later, I suspect that the characteristic of this need is that it can never be wholly clear to itself.

To try to describe it without distorting it we shall have to say something like this: Being is – or should be – necessary. It is impossible that everything should be reduced to a play of successive appearances which are inconsistent with each other ("inconsistent" is essential), or, in the words of Shakespeare, to "a tale told by an idiot." I aspire to participate in this being, in this reality – and perhaps this aspiration is already a degree of participation, however rudimentary.

Such a need, it may be noted, is to be found at the heart of the most inveterate pessimism. Pessimism has no meaning unless it signifies: it would surely be well if there were being, but there is no being, and I, who observe this fact, am therefore nothing.

As for defining the word "being," let us admit that it is extremely difficult. I would merely suggest this method of approach: being is what withstands – or what would withstand – an exhaustive analysis bearing on the data of experience and aiming to reduce them step by step to elements increasingly devoid of intrinsic or significant value. (An analysis of this kind is attempted in the theoretical works of Freud.)

When the pessimist Besme says in *La Ville* [by Claudel] that *nothing is*, he means precisely this, that there is no experience that withstands this analytical test. And it is always towards death regarded as the manifestation, the proof of this ultimate nothingness that the kind of inverted apologetic which arises out of absolute pessimism will inevitably gravitate.

A philosophy which refuses to endorse the ontological need is, nevertheless, possible; indeed, generally speaking, contemporary thought tends towards this abstention. But at this point a distinction must be made between two different attitudes which are sometimes confused: one which consists in a systematic reserve (it is that of agnosticism in all its forms), and the other, bolder and more coherent, which regards the ontological need as the expression of an outworn body of dogma liquidated once and for all by the Idealist critique.

The former appears to me to be purely negative: it is merely the expression of an intellectual policy of "not raising the question."

The latter, on the contrary, claims to be based on a positive theory of thought. This is not the place for a detailed critical study of this philosophy. I shall only note that it seems to me to tend towards an unconscious relativism or else towards a monism which ignores the personal in all its form, ignores the tragic and denies the transcendent, seeking to reduce it to its caricatural expressions which distort its essential character. I shall also point out that, just because this philosophy continually stresses the activity of verification, it ends by ignoring *presence* – that inward realization of presence through love which infinitely transcends all possible verification because it exists in an immediacy beyond all conceivable mediation. This will be clearer to some extent from what follows.

Thus I believe for my part that the ontological need cannot be silenced by an arbitrary dictatorial act which mutilates the life of the spirit at its roots. It remains true, nevertheless, that such an act is possible, and the conditions of our life are such that we can well believe that we are carrying it out; this must never be forgotten.

Being and Knowledge

These preliminary reflections on the ontological need are sufficient to bring out its indeterminate character and to reveal a fundamental paradox. To formulate this need is to raise a host of questions: Is there such a thing as being? What is it? etc. Yet immediately an abyss opens under my feet: I who ask these questions about being, how can I be sure that I exist?

Yet surely I, who formulate this *problem*, should be able to remain *outside it – before* or *beyond* it? Clearly this is not so. The more I consider it the more I find that this problem tends inevitably to invade the proscenium from which it is excluded in theory: it is only by means of a fiction that Idealism in its traditional form seeks to maintain on the margin of being the consciousness which asserts it or denies it.

So I am inevitably forced to ask: Who am I – I who question being? How am I qualified to begin this investigation? If I do not exist, how can I succeed in it? And if I do exist, how can I be sure of this fact?

Contrary to the opinion which suggests itself at this point, I believe that on this plane the *cogito* cannot help us at all. Whatever Descartes may have thought of it himself, the only certainty with which it provides us concerns only the epistemological subject as organ of objective cognition. As I have written elsewhere, the *cogito* merely guards the threshold of objective validity, and that is strictly all; this is proved by the indeterminate character of the I. The I *am* is, to my mind, a global statement which it is impossible to break down into its component parts.

There remains a possible objection; it might be said: Either the being designated in the question "What am I?" concerns the subject of cognition, and in this case we are on the plane of the *cogito;* or else that which you call the ontological need is merely the extreme point (or perhaps only the fallacious transposition) of a need which is, in reality, vital and with which the metaphysician is not concerned.

But is it not a mistake arbitrarily to divide the question, *Who am I?* from the ontological "problem" taken as a whole? The truth is that neither of the two can be dealt with separately, but that when they are taken together, they cancel one another out *as problems*.

It should be added that the Cartesian position is inseparable from a form of dualism which I, for my part, would unhesitatingly reject. To raise the ontological problem is to raise the question of being as a whole and of oneself seen as a totality.

But should we not ask ourselves if we must not reject this dissociation between the intellectual and the vital, with its resultant over- or under-estimation of the one or the other? Doubtless it is legitimate to establish certain distinctions within the unity of the being who thinks and who endeavors to *think himself;* but it is only beyond such distinctions that the ontological problem can arise and it must relate to that being seen in his all-comprehensive unity.

To sum up our reflections at this point, we find that we are dealing with an urge towards an affirmation – yet an affirmation which it seems impossible to make, since it is not until it has been made that I can regard myself as qualified to make it.

It should be noted that this difficulty never arises at a time when I am actually faced with a problem to be solved. In such a case I work on the data, but everything leads me to believe that I need not take into account the I who is at work – it is a factor which is presupposed and nothing more.

Here, on the contrary, what I would call the ontological status of the investigator assumes a decisive importance. Yet so long as I am concerned with thought itself I seem to follow an endless regression. But by the very fact of recognizing it as endless I transcend it in a certain way: I see that this process takes place within an affirmation of being – an affirmation which I *am* rather than an affirmation which I *utter:* by uttering it I break it, I divide it, I am on the point of betraying it.

It might be said, by way of an approximation, that my inquiry into being presupposes an affirmation in regard to which I am, in a sense, passive, *and of which I am the stage rather than the subject.* But this is only at the extreme limit of thought, a limit which I cannot reach without falling into contradiction. I am therefore led to assume or to recognize a form of participation which has the reality of a subject; this participation cannot be, by definition, an *object* of thought; it cannot serve as a solution – it appears beyond the realm of problems: it is meta-problematical.

Conversely, it will be seen that, if the meta-problematical can be asserted at all, it must be conceived as transcending the opposition between the subject who asserts the existence of being, on the one hand, and being *as asserted by that subject,* on the other, and as underlying it in a given sense. To postulate the meta-problematical is to postulate the primacy of being over knowledge (not of being as *asserted,* but of being as *asserting itself);* it is to recognize that knowledge is, as it were, environed by being, that it is interior to it in a certain sense – a sense perhaps analogous to that which Paul Claudel tried to define in his *Art Poetique.* From this standpoint, contrary to what epistemology seeks vainly to establish, there exists well and truly a mystery of cognition; knowledge is contingent on a participation in being for which no epistemology can account because it continually presupposes it.

Problem and Mystery: Concrete Examples

At this point we can begin to define the distinction between mystery and problem. A mystery is a problem which encroaches upon its own data, invading them, as it were, and thereby transcending itself as a simple problem. A set of examples will help us to grasp the content of this definition.

It is evident that there exists a mystery of the union of the body and the soul. The indivisible unity always inadequately expressed by such phrases as I *have a body*, I *make use of my body*, I *feel my body*, etc., can be neither analyzed nor reconstituted out of precedent elements. It is not only data, I would say that it is the basis of data, in the sense of being my own presence to myself, a presence of which the act of self-consciousness is, in the last analysis, only an inadequate symbol.

It will be seen at once that there is no hope of establishing an exact frontier between problem and mystery. For in reflecting on a mystery we tend inevitably to degrade it to the level of a problem. This is particularly clear in the case of the problem of evil.

In reflecting upon evil, I tend, almost inevitably, to regard it as a disorder which I view from outside and of which I seek to discover the causes or the secret aims. Why is it that the "mechanism" functions so defectively? Or is the defect merely apparent and due to a real defect of my vision? In this case the defect is in myself, yet it remains objective in relation to my thought, which discovers it and observes it. But evil which is only stated or observed is no longer evil which is suffered: in fact, it ceases to be evil. In reality, I can only grasp it as evil in the measure in which it *touches* me – that is to say, in the measure in which I am *involved*, as one is involved in a law-suit. Being "involved" is the fundamental fact; I cannot leave it out of account except by an unjustifiable fiction, for in doing so, I proceed as though I were God, and a God who is an onlooker at that.

This brings out how the distinction between what is *in me* and what is only *before me* can break down. This distinction falls under the blow of a certain kind of thought: thought at one remove.

But it is, of course, in love that the obliteration of this frontier can best be seen. It might perhaps even be shown that the domain of the meta-problematical coincides with that of love, and that love is the only starting point for the understanding of such mysteries as that of body and soul, which, in some manner, is its expression.

Actually, it is inevitable that, in being brought to bear on love, thought which has not thought itself – unreflected reflection – should tend to dissolve its meta-problematical character and interpret it in terms of abstract concepts, such as the will to live, the will to power, the *libido*, etc. On the other hand, since the domain of the problematical is that of the objectively valid, it will be extremely difficult – if not impossible – to refute these interpretations without changing to a new ground: a ground on which, to tell the truth, they lose their meaning. Yet I have the assurance, the certainty – and it envelops me like a protective cloak – that for as much as I really love I must not be concerned with these attempts at devaluation.

It will be asked: What is the criterion of true love? It must be answered that there is no criteriology except in the order of the objective and the problematical; but we can already see at a distance the eminent ontological value to be assigned to fidelity.

Let us take another illustration, more immediate and more particular, which may shed some light on the distinction between problem and mystery.

Say that I have made an encounter which has left a deep and lasting trace on all my life. It may happen to anyone to experience the deep spiritual significance of such a meeting – yet this is something which philosophers have commonly ignored or disdained, doubtless because it affects only the particular person as person – it cannot be universalized, it does not concern rational being in general.

It is clear that such a meeting raises, if you will, a problem; but it is equally clear that the solution of this problem will always fall short of the only question that matters. Suppose that I am told, for instance: "The reason you have met this person in this place is that you both like the same kind of scenery, or that you both need the same kind of treatment for your health" – the explanation means nothing. Crowds of people who apparently share my tastes were in the Engadine or in Florence at the time I was there; and there are always numbers of patients suffering from the same disease as myself at the health resort I frequent. But neither this supposed identity of tastes nor this common affliction has brought us together in any real sense; it has nothing to do with that intimate and unique affinity with which we are dealing. At the same time, it would be transgression of this valid reasoning to treat this affinity as if it were itself the cause and to say: "It is precisely this which has determined our meeting."

Hence I am in the presence of a mystery. That is to say, of a reality rooted in what is beyond the domain of the problematical properly so called. Shall we avoid the difficulty by saying that it was after all nothing but a coincidence, a lucky chance? But the whole of me immediately protests against this empty formula, this vain negation of what I apprehend with the deepest of my being. Once again we are brought back to our first definition of a mystery as a problem which encroaches upon its own data: I who inquire into the meaning and the possibility of this meeting, I cannot place myself outside it or before it; I am engaged in this encounter, I depend upon it, I am inside it in a certain sense, it envelops me and it comprehends me – even if it is not comprehended by me. Thus it is only by a kind of betrayal or denial that I can say: "After all, it might not have happened, I would still have been what I was, and what I am to-day." Nor must it be said: I have been changed by it as by an outward cause. No, it has developed me from within, it has acted in me as an inward principle.

But this is very difficult to grasp without distortion. I shall be inevitably tempted to react against this sense of the inwardness of the encounter, tempted by my probity itself, by what from a certain standpoint I must judge to be the best – or at least the safest – of myself.

An Objection

There is a danger that these explanations may strengthen in the minds of my readers a preliminary objection which must be stated at once.

It will be said: The meta-problematical of which you speak is after all a content of thought; how then should we not ask ourselves what is its mode of existence? What assures us of its existence at all? Is it not itself problematical in the highest degree?

My answer is categorical: To think, or, rather, to assert, the meta-problematical is to assert it as indubitably real, as a thing of which I cannot doubt without falling into contradiction. We are in a sphere where it is no longer possible to dissociate the idea itself from the certainty or the degree of certainty which pertains to it. Because this idea *is* certainty, it *is* the assurance of itself; it is, in this sense, something other and something more than an idea. As for the term *content of thought* which figured in the objection, it is deceptive in the highest degree. For content is, when all is said and done, derived from experience; whereas it is only by a way of liberation and detachment from experience that we can possibly rise to the level of the meta-problematical and of mystery. This liberation must be *real*; this detachment must be *real*; they must not be an abstraction, that is to say a fiction recognized as such.

Recollection

And this at last brings us to recollection, for it is in recollection and in this alone that this detachment is accomplished. I am convinced, for my part, that no ontology – that is to say, no apprehension of ontological mystery in whatever degree – is possible except to a being who is capable of recollecting himself, and of thus proving that he is not a living creature pure and simple, a creature, that is to say, which is at the mercy of its life and without a hold upon it.

It should be noted that recollection, which has received little enough attention from pure philosophers, is very difficult to define – if only because it transcends the dualism of being and action or, more correctly, because it reconciles in itself these two aspects of the antinomy. The word means what it says – the act whereby I re-collect myself as a unity; but this hold, this grasp upon myself, is also relaxation and abandon. *Abandon to . . . relaxation in the presence of . . .* yet there is no noun for these prepositions to govern. The way stops at the threshold.

Here, as in every other sphere, problems will be raised, and it is the psychologist who will raise them. All that must be noted is that the psychologist is no more in a position to shed light on the metaphysical bearing of recollection than on the noetic value of knowledge.

It is within recollection that I take up my position – or, rather, I become capable of taking up my position – in regard to my life; I withdraw from it in a certain way, but not as the pure subject of cognition; *in this withdrawal I carry with me that which I am and which perhaps my life is not.* This brings out the gap between my being and my life. I am not my life; and if I can judge my life – a fact I cannot deny without falling into a radical skepticism which is nothing other than despair – it is only on condition that I encounter myself within recollection beyond all possible judgment and, I would add, beyond all representation. Recollection is doubtless what is least spectacular in the soul; it does not consist in looking at something, it is an inward hold, an inward reflection, and it might be asked in passing whether it should not be seen as the ontological basis of memory – that principle of effective and non-representational unity on which the possibility of remembrance rests. The double meaning of "recollection" in English is revealing. It may be asked: is not recollection identical with that dialectical moment of the turning to oneself (*retour sur soi*) or else with the *fuer sich sein* which is the central theme of German Idealism?

I do not think so. To withdraw into oneself is not to be for oneself nor to mirror oneself in the intelligible unity of subject and object. On the contrary. I would say that here we come up against the paradox of that actual mystery whereby the I into which I withdraw ceases, for as much, to belong to itself. "You are not your own" – this great saying of St. Paul assumes in this connection its full concrete and ontological significance; it is the nearest approach to the reality for which we are groping. It will be asked: is not this reality an object of intuition? Is not that which you term "recollection" the same as what others have termed "intuition"?

But this again seems to me to call for the utmost prudence. If intuition can be mentioned in this context at all, it is not an intuition which is, or can be, given as such. The more an intuition is central and basic in the being whom it illuminates, the less it is capable of turning back and apprehending itself.

Moreover, if we reflect on what an intuitive knowledge of being could possibly be, we see that it could never figure in a collection, a procession of simple experiences or *Erlebnisse*, which all have this characteristic that they can be at times absorbed and at others isolated and, as it were, uncovered. Hence, any effort to remember such an intuition, to represent it to oneself, is inevitably fruitless. From this point of view, to be told of an intuitive knowledge of being is like being invited to play on a soundless piano. Such an intuition cannot be brought out into the light of day, for the simple reason that we do not possess it.

We are here at the most difficult point of our whole discussion. Rather than to speak of intuition in this context, we should say that we are dealing with an assurance which underlies the entire development of thought, even of discursive thought; it can therefore be approached only by a second reflection – a reflection whereby I ask myself how and from what starting point I was able to proceed in my initial reflection, which itself postulated the ontological, but without knowing it. This second reflection is recollection in the measure in which recollection can be self-conscious.

It is indeed annoying to have to use such abstract language in a matter which is not one of dialectics *ad usum philosophorum*, but of what is the most vital and, I would add, the most dramatic moment in the rhythm of consciousness seeking to be conscious of itself.

It is this dramatic aspect which must now be brought out.

Despair, and the Need for Being

Let us recall what we said earlier on: that the ontological need, the need of being, can deny itself. In a different context we said that being and life do not coincide; my life, and by reflection all life, may appear to me as for ever inadequate to something which I carry within me, which in a sense I am, but which reality rejects and excludes. Despair is possible in any form, at any moment and to any degree, and this betrayal may seem to be counseled, if not forced upon us, by the very structure of the world we live in. The deathly aspect of this world may, from a given standpoint, be regarded as a ceaseless incitement to denial and to suicide. It could even be said in this sense that the fact that suicide is always possible is the essential starting point of any genuine metaphysical thought.

It may be surprising to find in the course of this calm and abstract reasoning such verbal star turns – words so emotionally charged – as "suicide" and "betrayal." They are not a concession to sensationalism. I am convinced that it is in drama and through drama that metaphysical thought grasps and defines itself *in concreto.* Two years ago, in a lecture on the "Problem of Christian Philosophy" which he delivered at Louvain, M. Jacques Maritain said: "There is nothing easier for a philosophy than to become tragic, it has only to let itself go to its human weight." The allusion was doubtless to the speculation of a Heidegger. I believe, on the contrary, that the natural trend of philosophy leads it into a sphere where it seems that tragedy has simply vanished – evaporated at the touch of abstract thought. This is borne out by the work of many contemporary Idealists. Because they ignore the person, offering it up to I know not what ideal truth, to what principle of pure inwardness, they are unable to grasp those tragic factors of human existence to which I have alluded above; they banish them, together with illness and everything akin to it, to I know not what disreputable suburb of thought outside the ken of any philosopher worthy of the name. But, as I have stressed earlier on, this attitude is intimately bound up with the rejection of the ontological need; indeed, it is the same thing.

If I have stressed despair, betrayal and suicide, it is because these are the most manifest expressions of the will to negation as applied to being.

Let us take despair. I have in mind the act by which one despairs of reality as a whole, as one might despair of a person. This appears to be the result, or the immediate translation into other terms, of a kind of balance sheet. Inasmuch as I am able to evaluate the world of reality (and, when all is said and done, what I am unable to evaluate is for me as if it were not), I can find nothing in it that withstands that process of dissolution at the heart of things which I have discovered and traced. I believe that at the root of despair there is always this affirmation: "There is nothing in the realm of reality to which I can give credit – no security, no guarantee." It is a statement of complete insolvency.

Hope, and the Ontological Mystery

As against this, hope is what implies credit. Contrary to what was thought by Spinoza, who seems to me to have confused two quite distinct notions, fear is correlated to desire and not to hope, whereas what is negatively correlated to hope is the act which consists in putting things at their worst – an act which is strikingly illustrated by what is known as defeatism, and which is ever in danger of being degraded into the desire of the worst. Hope consists in asserting that there is at the heart of being, beyond all data, beyond all inventories and all calculations, a mysterious principle which is in connivance with me, which cannot but will that which I will, if what I will deserves to be willed and is, in fact, willed by the whole of my being.

We have now come to the center of what I have called the ontological mystery, and the simplest illustrations will be the best. To hope against all hope that a person whom I love will recover from a disease which is said to be incurable is to say: It is impossible that I should be alone in willing this cure; it is impossible that reality in its inward depth should be hostile or so much as indifferent to what I assert is in itself a good. It is quite useless to tell me of discouraging *cases* or *examples*: beyond all experience, all probability, all statistics, I assert that a given order shall be re-established, that reality is on my side in willing it to be so. I do not wish: I assert; such is the prophetic tone of true hope.

No doubt I shall be told: "In the immense majority of cases this is an illusion." But it is of the essence of hope to exclude the consideration of cases; moreover, it can be shown that there exists an ascending dialectic of hope, whereby hope rises to a plane which transcends the level of all possible empirical disproof – the plane of salvation as opposed to that of success in whatever form.

It remains true, nevertheless, that the correlation of hope and despair subsists until the end; they seem to me inseparable. I mean that while the structure of the world we live in permits – and may even seem to counsel – absolute despair, yet it is only such a world that can give rise to an unconquerable hope. If only for this reason, we cannot be sufficiently thankful to the great pessimists in the history of thought; they have carried through an inward experience which needed to be made and of which the radical possibility no apologetics should disguise; they have prepared our minds to understand that despair can be what it was for Nietzsche (though on an infra-ontological level and in a domain fraught with mortal dangers), the springboard to the loftiest affirmation.

At the same time, it remains certain that, for as much as hope is a mystery, its mystery can be ignored or converted into a problem. Hope is then regarded as a desire which wraps itself up in illusory judgments to distort an objective reality which it is interested in disguising from itself. What happens in this case is what we have already observed in connection with encounter and with love; it is because mystery can – and, in a sense, logically must – be degraded into a problem that an interpretation such as that of Spinoza, with all the confusion it implies, had to be put forward sooner or later. It is important and must be stressed that this attitude has nothing against it so long as our standpoint is on the hither-side of the realm of the ontological. Just as long as my attitude towards reality is that of someone who is not involved in it, but who judges it his duty to draw up its minutes as exactly as possible (and this is by definition the attitude of the scientist), I am justified in maintaining in regard to it a sort of principle of mistrust, which in theory is unlimited in its application; such is the legitimate standpoint of the workman in the laboratory, who must in no way prejudge the result of his analysis, and who can all the better envisage *the worst,* because at this level the very notion of worst is empty of meaning. But an investigation of this sort, which is just like that of an accountant going through the books, takes place on the hither-side of the order of mystery, an order in which the problem encroaches upon its own data.

It would indeed be a profound illusion to believe that I can still maintain this same attitude when I undertake an inquiry, say, into the value of life; it would be a paralogism to suppose that I can pursue such an inquiry as though my own life were not at issue.

Hence, between hope – the reality of hope in the heart of the one whom it inhabits – and the judgment brought to bear upon it by a mind chained to objectivity there exists the same barrier as that which separates a pure mystery from a pure problem.

This brings us to a nodal point of our subject, where certain intimate connections can be traced.

The world of the problematical is the world of fear and desire, which are inseparable; at the same time, it is that world of the functional – or of what can be functionalized – which was defined at the beginning of this essay; finally, it is the kingdom of technics of whatever sort. Every technique serves, or can be made to serve, some desire or some fear; conversely, every desire as every fear tends to invent its appropriate technique. From this standpoint, despair consists in the recognition of the ultimate inefficacy of all technics, joined to the inability or the refusal to change over to a new ground – a ground where all technics are seen to be incompatible with the fundamental nature of being, which itself escapes our grasp (in so far as our grasp is limited to the world of objects and to this alone). It is for this reason that we seem nowadays to have entered upon the very era of despair; we have not ceased to believe in technics, that is to envisage reality as a complex of problems; yet at the same time the failure of technics *as a whole* is as discernible to us as its *partial* triumphs. To the question: what can man achieve? we continue to reply: He can achieve as much as his technics; yet we are obliged to admit that these technics are unable *to save man himself,* and even that they are apt to conclude the most sinister alliance with the enemy he bears within him.

I have said that man is *at the mercy of his technics*. This must be understood to mean that he is increasingly incapable of controlling his technics, or rather of *controlling his own control*. This control of his own control, which is nothing else than the expression on the plane of active life of what I have called thought at one remove, cannot find its center or its support anywhere except in recollection.

It will be objected that even those whose faith in technics is strongest are bound to admit that there exist enormous realms which are outside man's control. But what matters is the spirit in which this admission is made. We have to recognize that we have no control over meteorological conditions, but the question is: do we consider it desirable and just that we should have such control? The more the sense of the ontological tends to disappear, the more unlimited become the claims of the mind which has lost it to a kind of cosmic governance, because it is less and less capable of examining its own credentials to the exercise of such dominion.

It must be added that the more the disproportion grows between the claims of the technical intelligence on the one hand, and the persisting fragility and precariousness of what remains its material substratum on the other, the more acute becomes the constant danger of despair which threatens this intelligence. From this standpoint there is truly an intimate dialectical correlation between the optimism of technical progress and the philosophy of despair which seems inevitably to emerge from it – it is needless to insist on the examples offered by the world of today.

It will perhaps be said: This optimism of technical progress is animated by great hope. How is hope in this sense to be reconciled with the ontological interpretation of hope?

I believe it must be answered that, *speaking metaphysically, the only genuine hope is hope in what does not depend on ourselves*, hope springing from humility and not from pride. This brings us to the consideration of another aspect of the mystery – a mystery which, in the last analysis, is one and unique – on which I am endeavoring to throw some light.

The metaphysical problem of pride – hubris – which was perceived by the Greeks and which has been one of the essential themes of Christian theology, seems to me to have been almost completely ignored by modern philosophers other than theologians. It has become a domain reserved for the moralist. Yet from my own standpoint it is an essential – if not the vital – question. It is sufficient to recall Spinoza's definition of *superbia* in his *Ethics* (III, def. XXVIII) to see how far he was from grasping the problem: "Pride is an exaggeratedly good opinion of ourselves which arises from self-love." In reality, this is a definition of vanity. As for pride, it consists in drawing one's strength solely from oneself. The proud man is cut off from a certain form of communion with his fellow men, which pride, acting as a principle of destruction, tends to break down. Indeed, this destructiveness can be equally well directed against the self; pride is in no way incompatible with self-hate; this is what Spinoza does not seem to have perceived.

A Second Objection

An important objection may be raised at the point we have now reached.

It will perhaps be said: Is not that which you are justifying ontologically in reality a kind of moral quietism which is satisfied by passive acceptance, resignation and inert hope? But what, then, becomes of man as man, as active being? Are we to condemn action itself inasmuch as it implies a self-confidence which is akin to pride? Can it be that action itself is a kind of degradation?

This objection implies a series of misunderstandings.

To begin with, the idea of inert hope seems to me a contradiction in terms. Hope is not a kind of listless waiting; it underpins action or it runs before it, but it becomes degraded and lost once the action is spent. Hope seems to me, as it were, the prolongation into the unknown of an activity which is central – that is to say, rooted in being. Hence it has affinities, not with desire, but with the will. The will implies the same refusal to calculate possibilities, or at any rate it suspends this calculation. Could not hope therefore be defined as the will when it is made to bear on what does not depend on itself?

The experimental proof of this connection is that it is the most active saints who carry hope to its highest degree; this would be inconceivable if hope were simply an inactive state of the soul. The mistake so often made here comes from a stoical representation of the will as a stiffening of the soul, whereas it is on the contrary relaxation and creation.

Creative Fidelity

The term "creation," which occurs here for the first time, is, nevertheless, decisive. Where there is creation there can be no degradation, and to the extent that technics are creative, or imply creativity, they are not degrading in any way. Degradation begins at the point where creativeness falls into self-imitation and self-hypnotism, stiffening and falling back on itself. This may, indeed, bring out the origin of the confusion which I denounced in the context of recollection.

Great is the temptation to confuse two distinct movements of the soul, whose opposition is blurred by the use of special metaphors. The stiffening, the contraction, the falling back on the self which are inseparable from pride, and which are indeed its symbol, must not be confused with the humble withdrawal which befits recollection and whereby I renew my contact with the ontological basis of my being.

There is every reason to think that such withdrawal in recollection is a presupposition of aesthetic creativity itself. Artistic creation, like scientific research, excludes the act of self-centering and self-hypnotism which is, ontologically speaking, pure negation.

It may perhaps seem that my thesis comes so near to that of Bergson as to coincide with it, but I do not think that this is the case. The terms almost invariably used by Bergson suggest that for him the essential character of creativity lay in its inventiveness, in its spontaneous innovation. But I wonder if by limiting our attention to this aspect of creation we do not lose sight of its ultimate significance, which is its deep-rootedness in being. It is at this point that I would bring in the notion of *creative fidelity;* it is a notion which is the more difficult to grasp and, above all, to define conceptually, because of its underlying and unfathomable paradox, and because it is at the very center of the realm of the meta-problematical.

It is important to note that the idea of fidelity seems difficult to maintain in the context of Bergsonian metaphysics, because it will tend to be interpreted as a routine, as an observance in the pejorative sense of the word, as an arbitrary safeguard *against* the power of renewal which is the spirit itself.

I am inclined to think that there is something in this neglect of the values of fidelity which deeply vitiates the notion of static religion as it is put forward in *Les Deux Sources de la Morale et de la Religion.* It may perhaps be useful to devote some thought to creative fidelity in order to elucidate this point.

Faithfulness is, in reality, the exact opposite of inert conformism. It is the active recognition of something permanent, not formally, after the manner of a law, but ontologically; in this sense, it refers invariably to a presence, or to something which can be maintained within us and before us as a presence, but which, *ipso facto,* can be just as well ignored, forgotten and obliterated; and this reminds us of that menace of betrayal which, to my mind, overshadows our whole world.

It may perhaps be objected that we commonly speak of fidelity to a principle. But it remains to be seen if this is not an arbitrary transposition of the notion of fidelity. A principle, in so far as it is a mere abstract affirmation, can make no demands upon me because it owes the whole of its reality to the act whereby I sanction it or proclaim it. Fidelity to a principle as a principle is idolatry in the etymological sense of the word; it might be a sacred duty for me to deny a principle from which life has withdrawn and which I know that I no longer accept, for by continuing to conform my actions to it, it is myself – myself as presence – that I betray.

So little is fidelity akin to the inertia of conformism that it implies an active and continuous struggle against the forces of interior dissipation, as also against the sclerosis of habit. I may be told: This is nevertheless no more than a sort of active conservation which is the opposite of creation. We must, I think, go much further into the nature of fidelity and of presence before we can reply to this point.

If presence were merely an *idea* in us whose characteristic was that it was nothing more than itself, then indeed the most we could hope would be to maintain this idea in us or before us, as one keeps a photograph on a mantelpiece or in a cupboard. But it is of the nature of presence as presence to be uncircumscribed; and this takes us once again beyond the frontier of the problematical. Presence is mystery in the exact measure in which it is presence. Now fidelity is the active perpetuation of presence, the renewal of its benefits – of its virtue which consists in a mysterious incitement to create. Here again we may be helped by the consideration of aesthetic creativeness; for if artistic creation is conceivable, it can only be on condition that the world is present to the artist in a certain way – present to his heart and to his mind, present to his very being.

Thus if creative fidelity is conceivable, it is because fidelity is ontological in its principle, because it prolongs presence which itself corresponds to a certain kind of hold which being has upon us; because it multiplies and deepens the effect of this presence almost unfathomably in our lives. This seems to me to have almost inexhaustible consequences, if only for the relationships between the living and the dead.

I must insist once again: A presence to which we are faithful is not at all the same thing as the carefully preserved effigy of an object which has vanished; an effigy is, when all is said and done, nothing but a likeness; metaphysically it is *less* than the object, it is a diminution of the object. Whereas presence, on the contrary, is *more* than the object, it exceeds the object on every side. We are here at the opening of a vista at whose term death will appear as the *test of presence*. This is an essential point and we must consider it carefully.

It will no doubt be said: What a strange way of denying death! Death *is* a phenomenon definable in biological terms; it is *not* a test.

It must be answered: It is what it signifies and, moreover, what it signifies to a being who rises to the highest spiritual level to which it is possible for us to attain. It is evident that if I read in the newspaper of the death of Mr. So-and-so, who is for me nothing but a name, this event is for me nothing more than the subject of an announcement. But it is quite another thing in the case of a being who has been granted to me as a presence. In this case, everything depends on me, on my inward attitude of maintaining this presence which could be debased into an effigy.

Further Objection

It will be objected: This is nothing more than a description in recondite and unnecessarily metaphysical terms of a common psychological fact. It is evident that it depends upon us in a certain measure to enable the dead to survive in our memory, but this existence is no more than subjective.

I believe that the truth is altogether different and infinitely more mysterious. In saying, "It depends upon us that the dead should live on in our memory," we are still thinking of the idea in terms of a diminution or an effigy. We admit that the object has disappeared, but that there remains a likeness which it is in our power to keep, as a daily woman "keeps" a flat or a set of furniture. It is all too evident that this manner of keeping can have no ontological value whatsoever. But it is altogether different in the case where fidelity is creative in the sense which I have tried to define. A presence is a reality; it is a kind of influx; it depends upon us to be permeable to this influx, but not, to tell the truth, to call it forth. Creative fidelity consists in maintaining ourselves actively in a permeable state; and there is a mysterious interchange between this free act and the gift granted in response to it.

An objection which is the converse of the preceding one may be expected at this point. I will be told: "All right. You have now ceased to decorate a psychological platitude with metaphysical ornaments, but only to make a gratuitous assertion which is unproved and which is beyond all possible experimental proof; this was inevitable as soon as you re-placed the ambiguous and neutral term 'presence' by the much more compromising term 'influx.'"

To reply to this objection, we must refer again to what I have already said of mystery and of recollection. Indeed, it is only on the meta-problematical level that the notion of influx can possibly be accepted. If it were taken in its objective sense, as an accretion of strength, we would indeed be faced with a thesis, not of metaphysics, but of physics, which would be open to every possible objection. When I say that a being is granted to me as a presence or as a being (it comes to the same, for he is not a being for me unless he is a presence), this means that I am unable to treat him as if he were merely placed in front of me; between him and me there arises a relationship which, in a sense, surpasses my awareness of him; he is not only before me, he is also within me – or, rather, these categories are transcended, they have no longer any meaning. The word influx conveys, though in a manner which is far too physical and special, the kind of interior accretion, of accretion from within, which comes into being as soon as presence is effective. Great and almost invincible is the temptation to think that such effective presence can be only that of an object; but if we believed this we would fall back to the level of the problematical and remain on the hither-side of mystery; and against this belief fidelity raises up its voice: "Even if I cannot see you, if I cannot touch you, I feel that you are with me; it would be a denial of you not to be assured of this." *With* me: note the metaphysical value of this word, so rarely recognized by philosophers, which corresponds neither to a relationship of inherence or immanence nor to a relationship of exteriority. It is of the essence of genuine *coesse* – I must use the Latin word – that is to say, of genuine intimacy, to lend itself to the decomposition to which it is subjected by critical thought; but we already know that there exists another kind of thought, a thought which bears upon that thought itself, and is related to a bottled up yet efficacious underlying intuition, of which it suffers the attraction.

Spiritual Availability and Presence

It must be added (and this brings us to the verge of another sphere) that the value of such intimacy, particularly in regard to the relation between the living and the dead, will be the higher and the more assured the more this intimacy is grounded in the realm of total spiritual availability (*disponibilité*) – that is to say, of pure charity; and I shall note in passing that an ascending dialectic of creative fidelity corresponds to the dialectic of hope to which I have already referred. The notion of availability is no less important for our subject than that of presence, with which it is bound up.

It is an undeniable fact, though it is hard to describe in intelligible terms, that there are some people who reveal themselves as "present" – that is to say, at our disposal – when we are in pain or in need to confide in someone, while there are other people who do not give us this feeling, however great is their goodwill. It should be noted at once that the distinction between presence and absence is not at all the same as that between attention and distraction. The most attentive and the most conscientious listener may give me the impression of not being present; he gives me nothing, he cannot make room for me in himself, whatever the material favors which he is prepared to grant me. The truth is that there is a way of listening which is a way of giving, and another way of listening which is a way of refusing, of refusing *oneself;* the material gift, the visible action, do not necessarily witness to presence. We must not speak of proof in this connection; the word would be out of place. Presence is something which reveals itself immediately and unmistakably in a look, a smile, an intonation or a handshake.

It will perhaps make it clearer if I say that the person who is at my disposal is the one who is capable of being with me with the whole of himself when I am in need; while the one who is not at my disposal seems merely to offer me a temporary loan raised on his resources. For the one I am a presence; for the other I am an object. Presence involves a reciprocity which is excluded from any relation of subject to object or of subject to subject-object. A concrete analysis of unavailability (*indisponibilité*) is no less necessary for our purpose than that of betrayal, denial or despair.

Unavailability is invariably rooted in some measure of alienation. Say, for instance, that I am told of some misfortune with which I am asked to sympathize: I understand what I am told; I admit in theory that the sufferers deserve my sympathy; I see that it is a case where it would be logical and just for me to respond with sympathy; I even offer my sympathy, but only with my mind; because, when all is said and done, I am obliged to admit that I feel absolutely nothing. Indeed, I am sorry that this should be so; the contradiction between the indifference which I feel in fact and the sympathy which I know I ought to feel is humiliating and annoying; it diminishes me in my own eyes. But it is no use; what remains in me is the rather embarrassing awareness that, after all, these are people I do not know – if one had to be touched by every human misfortune life would not be possible, it would indeed be too short. The moment I think: After all, this is only a case, No. 75,627, it is no good, I can feel nothing.

But the characteristic of the soul which is present and at the disposal of others is that it cannot think in terms of *cases*; in its eyes there are *no cases at all.*

And yet it is clear that the normal development of a human being implies an increasingly precise and, as it were, automatic division between what concerns him and what does not, between things for which he is responsible and those for which he is not. Each one of us becomes the center of a sort of mental space arranged in concentric zones of decreasing interest and participation. It is as though each one of us secreted a kind of shell which gradually hardened and imprisoned him; and this sclerosis is bound up with the hardening of the categories in accordance with which we conceive and evaluate the world.

Fortunately, it can happen to anyone to make an encounter which breaks down the framework of this egocentric topography; I know by my own experience how, from a stranger met by chance, there may come an irresistible appeal which overturns the habitual perspectives just as a gust of wind might tumble down the panels of a stage set – what had seemed near becomes infinitely remote and what had seemed distant seems to be close. Such cracks are repaired almost at once. But it is an experience which leaves us with a bitter taste, an impression of sadness and almost of anguish; yet I think it is beneficial, for it shows us as in a flash all that is contingent and – yes – artificial in the crystallized pattern of our personal system.

But it is, above all, the sanctity realized in certain beings which reveals to us that what we call the normal order is, from a higher point of view, from the standpoint of a soul rooted in ontological mystery, merely the subversion of an order which is its opposite. In this connection, the study of sanctity with all its concrete attributes seems to me to offer an immense speculative value; indeed, I am not far from saying that it is the true introduction to ontology.

Once again a comparison with the soul which is not at the disposal of others will throw light on our subject. To be incapable of presence is to be in some manner not only occupied but encumbered with one's own self. I have said in some manner; the immediate object of the preoccupation may be one of any number; I may be preoccupied with my health, my fortune, or even with *my inward perfection.* This shows that to be occupied with oneself is not so much to be occupied with *a particular object* as to be occupied in a *particular manner.* It must be noted that the contrary of this state is not a state of emptiness or indifference. The real contrast is rather between the being who is opaque and the being who is transparent. But this inward opacity remains to be analyzed. I believe that it consists in a kind of obduracy or fixation; and I wonder if, by generalizing and adapting certain psychoanalytical data, we would not find that it is the fixation in a given zone or in a given key of a certain disquiet which, in itself, is something quite different. But what is remarkable is that the disquiet persists within this fixation and gives it that character of constriction which I mentioned in connection with the degradation of the will. There is every reason to believe that this indefinite disquiet should be identified with the anguish of temporality and with that aspiration of man not towards, but *by* death, which is at the heart of pessimism.

Pessimism is rooted in the same soil as the inability to be at the disposal of others. If the latter grows in us as we grow old, it is only too often because, as we draw near to what we regard as the term of our life, anxiety grows in us almost to the point of choking us; to protect itself, it sets up an increasingly heavy, exacting and, I would add, vulnerable mechanism of self-defense. The capacity to hope diminishes in proportion as the soul becomes increasingly chained to its experience and to the categories which arise from it, and as it is given over more completely and more desperately to the world of the problematical.

Here at last can be brought together the various motifs and thematic elements which I have had to bring out one by one. In contrast to the captive soul we have described, the soul which is at the disposal of others is consecrated and inwardly dedicated; it is protected against suicide and despair, which are interrelated and alike, because it knows that it is not its own, and that the most legitimate use it can make of its freedom is precisely to recognize that it does not belong to itself; this recognition is the starting point of its activity and creativeness.

The difficulties of a philosophy of this sort must not be disguised. It is inevitably faced by a disquietening alternative: Either it will try to solve these difficulties – to give all the answers; in that case it will fall into the excesses of a dogmatism which ignores its vital principles and, I would add, into those of a sacrilegious theodicy, or else it will allow these difficulties to subsist, labeling them as mysteries.

Between these two I believe that there exists a middle way – a narrow, difficult and dangerous path which I have tried to discover. But, like Karl Jaspers in his *Philosophy of Existence*, I can only proceed in this kind of country by calling out to other travelers. If, as it occasionally happened, certain minds respond – not the generality, but this being and that other – then there is a way. But, as I believe Plato perceived with incomparable clarity, it is a way which is undiscoverable except through love, to which alone it is visible, and this brings us to what is perhaps the deepest characteristic of that realm of the meta-problematical of which I have tried to explore certain regions.

The Relation of this Philosophy to Christianity

A serious objection remains to be mentioned. It will perhaps be said: All that you have said implies an unformulated reference to the data of Christianity and can only be understood in the light of these data. Thus we understand what you mean by presence if we think of the Eucharist and what you mean by creative fidelity if we think of the Church. But what can be the value of such a philosophy for those who are a-Christian – for those who ignore Christianity or who do not accept it? I would answer: it is quite possible that the existence of the fundamental Christian data may be necessary *in fact* to enable the mind to conceive some of the notions which I have attempted to analyze; but these notions cannot be said to depend on the data of Christianity, and *they do not presuppose it.* On the other hand, should I be told that the intellect must leave out of account anything which is not a universal data of thinking as such, I would say that this claim is exaggerated and in the last analysis, illusory. Now, as at any other time, the philosopher is placed in a given historical situation from which he is most unlikely to abstract himself completely; he would deceive himself if he thought that he could create a complete void both within and around himself. Now this historical situation implies as one of its essential data the existence of the Christian fact – quite independently of whether the Christian religion is accepted and its fundamental assertions are regarded as true or false. What appears to me evident is that we cannot reason today as though there were not behind us centuries of Christianity, just as, in the domain of the theory of knowledge, we cannot pretend that there have not been centuries of positive science. But neither the existence of Christianity nor that of positive science plays in this connection more than the role of a fertilizing principle. It favors the development of certain ideas which we might not have conceived without it. This development may take place in what I would call paraChristian zones; for myself, I have experienced it more than twenty years before I had the remotest thought of becoming a Catholic.

Speaking more particularly to Catholics, I should like to note that from my own standpoint the distinction between the natural and the supernatural must be rigorously maintained. It will perhaps be objected that there is a danger that the word "mystery" might confuse this very issue. I would reply that there is no question of confusing those mysteries which are enveloped in human experience as such with those mysteries which are revealed, such as the Incarnation or Redemption, and to which no effort of thought bearing on experience can enable us to attain.

It will be asked: why then do you use the same word for two such distinct notions? But I would point out that no revelation is, after all, conceivable unless it is addressed to a being who is *involved – committed* – in the sense which I have tried to define – that is to say, to a being who participates in a reality which is non-problematical and which provides him with his foundation as subject. Supernatural life *must*, when all is said and done, find a hold in the natural – which is not to say that it is the flowering of the natural. On the contrary it seems to me that any study of the notion of *created Nature*, which is fundamental for the Christian, leads to the conclusion that there is in the depth of Nature, as of reason which is governed by it, a fundamental principle of inadequacy to itself which is, as it were, a restless anticipation of a different order.

To sum up my position on this difficult and important point, I would say that the recognition of the ontological mystery, in which I perceive as it were the central redoubt of metaphysics, is, no doubt, only possible through a sort of radiation which proceeds from revelation itself and which is perfectly well able to affect souls who are strangers to all positive religion of whatever kind; that this recognition, which takes place through certain higher modes of human experience, in no way involves the adherence to any given religion; but it enables those who have attained to it to perceive the possibility of a revelation in a way which is not open to those who have never ventured beyond the frontiers of the realm of the problematical and who have therefore never reached the point from which the mystery of being can be seen and recognized. Thus, a philosophy of this sort is carried by an irresistible movement towards the light which it perceives from afar and of which it suffers the secret attraction. [PE, pp. 9–46; essay first published in 1933]

*   *   *

2. Critique of Descartes, the Cogito, and Skepticism

I maintain – and this is a cardinal point – that, in the *I think* and in the *I believe*, the subject does not play one and the same part. I have said that the ego is the medium of freedom, that is to say, with the cogito the ego expresses the act by which freedom posits itself. But this ego is universal, or it is at least suppressed in the universality of the thinking subject. Inasmuch as I think, I am universal, and, if knowledge is dependent on the cogito, that is precisely in virtue of the universality inherent in the thinking ego. In faith there is nothing of the kind. It is precisely the absence of this clear distinction that causes the equivocations which have always played around the idea of a "*Vernunftrereligion*." [religion within the bounds of reason]. . . . The subject of faith is not thought in general. Thought in general in so far as it is reflected (and, as a result, is objectified) appears to itself as purely abstract, purely indeterminate, a formal condition and nothing more. The subject of faith, on the contrary, must be concrete. [MJ, p. 40]

*   *   *

Perhaps it will be objected that all I have said so far is really more posited than proved. I am perfectly ready to agree about this, as I consider that the very idea of bringing a demonstration to bear on the primacy of existence seems to me radically contradictory. Our only possible procedure here consists in reflecting on affirmations whose titles of credit, so to speak, need to be examined.

That existence cannot be treated as a *demonstrandum* is something that we cannot fail to perceive as soon as we observe that existence is primary or it is not – that in no case can it be regarded as capable of being reduced or derived. Nor is the affirmation of being of the order of the *principles* which we reach by way of regression. For principles only obtain in the infra- or supra- existential world from which precisely we are trying to escape. Thus we are confronted with an assurance which coincides closely with the reality on which it bears, a reality that is as global as the assurance itself. Here once again I am constrained to put the reader on his guard against the terms I need to use. For in the words "bear on" there is something that is not strictly applicable here, something that can only be applied to a judgment. We posit that a judgment refers to an object distinct from itself, that it points it out as an index does. But here there is no question of referring. In this respect I would be prepared to admit that the fundamental assurance we are dealing with here is of the order of sentiment or feeling – provided it were explicitly understood that this feeling must not be intellectualized and converted into a judgment, for any such conversion would not only change its nature but possibly even deprive it of all meaning.

Hence the distinction between the idea of existence and existence itself – an impasse in which philosophical reflection is always liable to get lost – must be rejected out of hand. I myself am unable to view this distinction as anything more than a fiction that derives its birth from the arbitrary act by which thought claims to transform into an affirmation of objectivity what is really immediate apprehension and participation. . . .

What I have already said is doubtless enough to enable the reader to discern the position that we are obliged to adopt regarding the cogito of Descartes. The reality that the cogito reveals – though without discovering an analytical basis for it – is of quite a different order from the existence that we are trying here not so much to *establish* as to *identify* in the sense of taking note of its absolute metaphysical priority. The cogito introduces us into a whole system of affirmations and guarantees their validity. *It guards the threshold of the valid* and it is only on condition that we identify the valid and the real that we can speak without the imprudence that is far too common – of the real as immanent in the act of thinking. Here, of course, we are in no way re-establishing an outworn distinction between matter and form. I have no hesitation in saying that the cogito is precisely the negation of this distinction and in some way the very act by which it is suppressed. But it certainly does not follow from this that the objective world to which access is opened up to us by the cogito coincides with the world of existence. The dualism established by Kant between the object and the thing-in-itself, whatever objections it raises in the form in which he states it in the *Critique*, has at least had the inestimable advantage of accustoming people's minds for over a century to making this indispensable dissociation. But it is important to be very clear in our minds that the existent can in no way be treated as an unknowable object, that is to say, as an object liberated from the very conditions that define an object as such. It is essential to the character of the *existent* that it should occupy with regard to thought a *position* which cannot be reduced to the position implied in the fact of objectivity itself. [MJ, pp. 324–326]

*   *   *

It may be said in this respect that no concrete philosophy is possible without a constantly renewed yet creative tension between the I and those depths of our being in and by which we are; nor without the most stringent and rigorous reflection, directed on our most intensely lived experience. . . . In general, the cogito in its idealist interpretation – I shall not decide whether it can be taken in any other sense – does not seem to me a likely point of departure for a possible metaphysics. . . . I have always strongly emphasized the fact that a philosophy which begins with the *cogito*, i.e., with non-commitment even if construed as an act, runs the risk of never getting back to being. "The incarnation is the datum with respect to which a fact becomes a possible"; it is not a form, and it cannot be maintained that it is a pure and simple relation. It is a datum which is not transparent to itself. The truth is that the seductiveness of the *cogito* for philosophers lies precisely in its apparent transparency. It is always appropriate to ask, however, whether this isn't a false supposition of transparency. This, I believe, creates a dilemma: either this supposition of transparency is false, and there is, as I believe, in the *cogito* itself an element of obscurity which cannot be elucidated – or, if the *cogito* is really transparent to itself, we can never infer existence from it no matter what logical procedures we use. At this point opacity and the conditions which cause it should become the object of our reflection. . . .[CF, pp. 65–66]

* * *

Even admitting that I do exist, how can I be assured that I do? In spite of the thought which comes first into my head, I do not think that Descartes' *cogito* can be of any help to us here. The *cogito* . . . is at the mere threshold of validity; the subject of the cogito is the epistemological subject. Cartesianism implies a severance, which may be fatal anyhow, between intellect and life; its result is a depreciation of the one, and an exaltation of the other, both arbitrary. There is here an inevitable rhythm only too familiar to us, for which we are bound to find an explanation. It would certainly not be proper to deny the legitimacy of making distinctions of order within the unity of a living subject, who thinks and strives to think of himself. But the ontological problem can only arise beyond such distinctions, and for the living being grasped in his full unity and vitality. [BH, pp. 170–171]

* * *

3. Feeling and Sensation, and Embodiment

So much for body as object: it seems, on the other hand, impossible to insist on what is specifically mine in my body without putting one's emphasis on the notion of feeling as such. Feeling, my feeling, is really what belongs only to me, my prerogative. What I feel is indissolubly linked to the fact that my body is my body, not just one body among others. I am out, let us say, for a walk with a friend. I say I feel tired. My friend looks skeptical, since he, for his part, feels no tiredness at all. I say to him, perhaps a little irritably, that nobody who is not inside my skin can know what I feel. He will be forced to agree, and yet, of course, he can always claim that I am attaching too much importance to slight disagreeable sensations which he, if he felt them, would resolutely ignore. It is all too clear that at this level no real discussion is possible.

For I can always say that even if what he calls "the same sensations" were felt by him and not by me, still, they would not really be, in their new setting, in the context of so many other sensations and feelings that I do not share, the same sensations; and that therefore his statement is meaningless. . . .

In so far, then, as we cling to the data of primary reflection, we cannot help thinking of sensation as some stimulus sent from an unknown source in outer space and intercepted by what we call a "subject," but a subject, in this case, thought of objectively, that is, as a physical receiving apparatus; in other words we think of sensation on the model of the emission and reception of a message. It is difficult, almost impossible, for a mind at the stage of primary reflection to deny that what is sent out at point x (that is to say, somewhere or other), then transmitted through space under conditions of which physics claims to give us an intelligible picture, is finally received and transcribed by the sensitive subject – transcribed, of course, in the key of the sense concerned. In short, we can hardly avoid thinking of sensation as the way in which a transmitter and a receiver communicate with each other and in this case . . . the imaginary model that conditions our thinking is that of a system of radio telegraphy. . . .

What does translation really consist of? Of the substitution of a set of given elements for another set of given elements, at least partly different in kind; however many differences there may be between the two sets, we should specially notice that both sets must be objective, that is, fully accessible to the mind. . . .

Now in the case of sensation, just nothing at all of this sort, or even remotely comparable to this, takes place. If I want to exercise the activity of a translator, I must start with a given something to work on, the text I am to translate from. This is a sort of prior datum: but the physical event prior to sensation, which I am supposed to be translating into the language of sensation, cannot be said to be a datum of mine in any sense whatsoever. If we do not at first acknowledge this fact, it is because we are spellbound by physical science's picture of some distant stimulus traveling towards the organism and shaking it up, and we confuse that conceptual picture with the fact of having an objective datum. What we are really doing is to project, in physical terms, the mysterious relationship which the term datum implies. But if we feel we must be more stringent in our reasoning than this, we are soon caught in a dilemma: either on the one hand, we must acknowledge that the physical event as such is not a datum of ours, is not, whatever modifications it may exercise on our bodies in so far as the latter too are considered in a purely objective fashion, *literally* given to us in any sense at all, in which case it seems impossible that this non-given physical event should ever be transformed into sense data; or on the other hand we shall have to bridge the gap between physical events and sense data by postulating the existence of an intermediary order of sensibilia, or unsensed sensa – of things that are like sensations in all respects, except that nobody is aware of them. . . . How are we to understand the notion of sensation which is a sensation in all respects, except that nobody is aware of it? If we stick to the general lines of the interpretation we started with, we shall have to treat the unsensed sensum as itself a message sent out from an emission post (but missing, in this case, its destination at the reception post), and then we are back where we started. Or, on the other hand, we can, of course, treat the unsensed sensum, or the sensibilium, as something primary and unanalysable; in that case, of course, it cannot be a message, and so the interpretation of sensation we started with has foundered. . . .

Secondary reflection is forced to recognize that our primary assumptions must be called in question, and that sensation, as such, should certainly not be conceived on the analogy of the transmission and reception of a message. For, and this is our basic reason for rejecting the analogy, every kind of message, however transmitted or received, presupposes the existence of sensation – exactly in the way in which, as we have already seen, every kind of instrument or apparatus presupposes the existence of my body. . . .

But as soon as we bring into the argument my body, in so far as it is my body, or the feeling which is not separable from my body as mine, our perspective changes, and we have to recognize the need to postulate the existence of what I will call a *non-mediatizable immediate*, which is the very root of our existence. This is a very difficult notion; and intelligence must simply bombard this non-mediatizable immediate with its rays if we are to have more than a dark and groping awareness of its whereabouts. . . . [MBI, pp. 104–108]

*   *   *

When I affirm that something exists, I always mean that I consider this something as connected with my body, as able to be put in contact with it, however indirect this contact may be. But note must be taken that the priority I thus ascribe to my body depends on the fact that my body is given to me in a way that is not exclusively objective, i.e., on the fact that it is my body. This character, at once mysterious and intimate, of the bond between me and my body (I purposely avoid the word relation) does in fact color all existential judgments. What it comes to is this: we cannot really separate: 1. Existence; 2. Consciousness of self as existing; 3. Consciousness of self as bound to a body, as incarnate.

From this several important conclusions would seem to follow: (1) In the first place, the existential point of view about reality cannot, it seems, be other than that of an incarnate personality. In so far as we can imagine a pure understanding, there is, for such an understanding, no possibility of considering things as existent or non-existent.

(2) On the one hand, the problem of the existence of the external world is now changed and perhaps even loses its meaning; I cannot in fact without contradiction think of my body as non-existent, since it is in connection with it (in so far as it is *my* body) that every existing thing is defined and placed. On the other hand, we ought to ask whether there are valid reasons for giving my body a privileged metaphysical status in comparison with other things.

(3) If this is so, it is permissible to ask whether the union of the soul and body is, in essence, really different from the union between the soul and other existing things. In other words, does not a certain experience of the self, as tied up with the universe, underlie all affirmation of existence?

(4) Inquire whether such an interpretation of the existential leads towards subjectivism. . . .

Incarnation—the central "given" of metaphysic. Incarnation is the situation of a being who appears to himself to be, as it were, *bound* to a body. This "given" is opaque to itself: opposition to the *cogito*. Of this body, I can neither say that it is I, nor that it is not I, nor that it is *for* me (object). The opposition of subject and object is found to be transcended from the start. Inversely, if I start from the opposition, treating it as fundamental, I shall find no trick of logical sleight of hand which lets me get back to the original experience, which will inevitably be either eluded or (which comes to the same thing) refused. We are not to object that this experience shows a contingent character: in point of fact, all metaphysical inquiry requires a starting-point of this kind. It can only start from a situation which is mirrored but cannot be understood. (BH, pp. 10–12)

*   *   *

What exactly is the meaning and value of the [phrase "my body"]? We will find insoluble difficulties no matter what way we try to explain it. Should I maintain, for example, as I have been tempted to do many times before, that my body is my instrument? If so, we must start by examining the instrumental relation. It seems plain that any instrument is a means of extending, developing, or strengthening an original power possessed by the person who uses it; this holds for a knife as much as for a lens. These powers or aptitudes are active properties of an organic body. If I consider my body from the outside, I can evidently think of it as a mechanism or as an instrument. But we are now examining the nature of my body insofar as it is mine. This body (*hoc corpus* not *illud*), this instrumentalist, can I construe it as itself an instrument – and if so, of what? It is clear that there is the danger of an infinite regress; if the instrumentalist is itself an instrument, of what is it the instrument, etc.? If I think of my body as an instrument, I thereby ascribe to the soul of which it is the instrument, as it were, those potentialities which the body ordinarily realizes; thus the soul is converted into a body and the same regress will now occur in connection with the soul. . . .

Does I and my body mean: I am identical with my body? Can this identity be maintained in the light of reflection? Clearly not. The alleged identity is absurd; it is possible to affirm it only if the I is first implicitly denied, thereby becoming the materialist assertion: my body is myself, only my body exists. But this assertion is absurd. For it is a property of my body that it does not and cannot exist alone. . . .

To be incarnated is to appear to oneself as body, as this particular body, without being identified with it nor distinguished from it – identification and distinction being correlative operations which are significant only in the realm of objects.

What clearly emerges from the foregoing reflections is the fact that there is no distinct haven to which I can repair either outside or within my body. Disincarnation is not practically possible and is precluded by my very structure.

However, there is a counterpart to the above which should be emphasized.

If I abstract from the index characterizing my body – insofar as it is mine – if I construe it as one body among an unlimited number of other such bodies, I will be forced to treat it as an object, as exhibiting the fundamental properties of objectivity. It then becomes an object of scientific knowledge; it becomes problematic, so to speak, but only on condition that I consider it as not-mine; and this detachment, which is essentially illusory, is the very basis of all cognition. As knowing subject, I re-establish or claim to reestablish that dualism between my body and me, that interval which, we have learned, is inconceivable from an existential point of view. A subject of this kind can be established only if existence is first renounced; it is, it can be said, only on condition that it considers itself not to be. This paradox is fundamental for the object, for I can really think about the object only if I acknowledge that I do not count for it, that it does not take me into account. This is the only valid response – and it is decisive – that can be made to the annoying question asked by empirical idealism; can objects continue to exist when I no longer perceive them? The truth is that they are objects only on that condition. . . .

On the one hand, the capacity I have to perceive my body to a certain extent from the outside (for example, figuratively, as when I see myself in a mirror) invariably tempts me to divorce myself from it ideally and to disavow it. . . . On the other hand, reflection detects the fallacious nature of such a divorce; as we have noted, reflection compels me to acknowledge that this separate entity, this self relative to which the possession of this particular body is accidental, cannot be thought of either in isolation or in relation, nor yet as identical with that from which I claim to separate it.

I should note in passing that such a reflection of the second degree or power whose object is another original reflection, is to my mind synonymous with philosophy itself viewed as an effort to restore the concrete beyond the disconnected and discontinuous determinations of abstract thought. . . .

The premises of what I venture to call concrete or existential philosophy have thus been established in a somewhat indirect – and unexpected way.

This philosophy is based on a datum which is not transparent to reflection, and which, when reflected, implies an awareness not of contradiction but of a fundamental mystery, becoming an antimony as soon as discursive thought tries to reduce or problematize it. . . . Existence, or better, existentiality, if I may be allowed to use this barbarism, is participation insofar as participation cannot be objectified. . . . It is only too clear that we irresistibly tend to objectify this participation and to construe it as a relation; it is only our free act which intervenes to prevent us. Our essential immediacy is disclosed in this act alone, and our discovery of it may occur in rather different areas which nevertheless communicate with one another – the areas of metaphysics, poetry, and art. [CF, pp. 18–24]

*　　*　　*

It is not, I think, very difficult to see that my link with my body is really the model (a model not shaped, but felt) to which I relate all kinds of ownership, for instance my ownership of my dog; but it is not true that this link can *itself* be defined as a sort of ownership. In other words it is by what literally must be called a paralogism that I seek to think through my relationship with my body, starting off with my relationship with my dog. The truth is rather that *within* every ownership, every kind of ownership I exercise, there is this kernel that I feel to be there at the center; and this kernel is nothing other than the experience – an experience which of its very nature cannot be formulated in intellectual terms – by which my body is mine. . . .

I cannot avoid being tempted to think of my body as a kind of instrument; or, more generally speaking, as the apparatus which permits me to act upon, and even to intrude myself into, the world. . . . Only let us remember that it is not *a* body, but *my* body, that we are asking ourselves questions about. As soon as we get back to this perspective . . . the whole picture changes.

My body is *my* body just in so far as I do *not* consider it in this detached fashion, do not put a gap between myself and it. To put this point in another way, my body is mine in so far as for me my body is not an object but, rather, I *am* my body. Certainly, the meaning of "am" in that sentence is, at a first glance, obscure; it is essentially, perhaps, in its implications, a negative meaning. To say that I am my body is to negate, to deny, to erase that gap which, on the other hand, I would be postulating as soon as I asserted that my body was merely my instrument. . . .

. . . The proper position to take up seems, on the contrary, to be this: I *am* my body in so far as I succeed in recognizing that this body of mine *cannot*, in the last analysis, be brought down to the level of being this object, *an* object, a something or other. It is at this point that we have to bring in the idea of the body not as an object but as a subject. It is in so far as I enter into some kind of relationship (though relationship is not an adequate term for what I have in mind) with the body, some kind of relationship which resists being made wholly objective to the mind, that I can properly assert that I am identical with me body. . . .

It goes without saying, by the way, that the term "incarnation," of which I shall have to make a frequent use from now on, applies solely and exclusively in our present context to the situation of a being who appears to himself to be linked fundamentally and not accidentally to *his* or *her* body. . . .

. . . my body, in so far as it is properly mine, presents itself to me in the first instance as something felt; I am my body only in so far as I am a being that has feelings. From this point of view it seems, therefore, that my body is endowed with an absolute priority in relation to everything that I can feel that is other than my body itself . . . [MBI, pp. 97–101]

*   *   *

4. Primary and Secondary Reflection

If I take experience as merely a sort of passive recording of impressions, I shall never manage to understand how the reflective process could be integrated with experience. On the other hand, the more we grasp the notion of experience in its proper complexity, in its active and I would even dare to say in its dialectical aspects, the better we shall understand how experience cannot fail to transform itself into reflection, and we shall even have the right to say that the more richly it is experience, the more, also, it is reflection. But we must, at this point, take one step more and grasp the fact that reflection itself can manifest itself at various levels; there is primary reflection, and there is also what I shall call secondary reflection; this secondary reflection has, in fact, been very often at work during these early lectures, and I dare to hope that as our task proceeds it will appear more and more clearly as the special high instrument of philosophical research. Roughly, we can say that where primary reflection tends to dissolve the unity of experience which is first put before it, the function of secondary reflection is essentially recuperative; it reconquers that unity. But how is such a reconquest possible? The possibility is what we are going to try to show by means of the quite general, the (in the parliamentary sense) privileged, example on which we must now concentrate our attention. We shall soon see that what we have to deal with here is not merely, in fact, an illustration or an example, but an actual way of access to a realm that is assuredly as near to us as can be, but that, nevertheless, by a fatality (a perfectly explicable fatality, however), has been, through the influence of modern thought, set at a greater and greater distance from us; so that the realm has become more and more of a problematic realm, and we are forced to call its very existence into question. I am talking about the self, about that reality of the self, with which we have already come into contact so often, but always to be struck by its disquieting ambiguity. [MBI, p. 83]

*   *   *

. . . Existence and the exclamatory awareness of existence cannot really be separated . . . we are . . . in the presence of a key datum, or rather a datum on which everything else hinges; we should also acknowledge from the first that this datum is not transparent to itself; nothing could bear a smaller likeness to the transcendental ego, which already in a certain sense in Kant's case, and much more notably among his successors, had taken its stance, as it were, at the heart and center of the philosophical arena.

This non-transparency . . . cannot be asserted apart from the datum . . . [of] my body: my body in so far as it is *my* body, my body in so far as it has the character, in itself so mysterious. . . .

Let us note at once that there could be no clearer example than that which we are now beginning to consider of the special part played in thought by secondary, by what I have called recuperative, reflection. Primary reflection, on the contrary, for its part, is forced to break the fragile link between me and my body that is constituted here by the word "mine." The body that I call my body is in fact only one body among many others. In relation to these other bodies, it has been endowed with no special privileges whatsoever. It is not enough to say that this is objectively true, it is the precondition of any sort of objectivity whatsoever, it is the foundation of all scientific knowledge (in the case we are thinking of, of anatomy, of physiology, and all their connected disciplines). Primary reflection is therefore forced to take up an attitude of radical detachment, of complete lack of interest, towards the fact that this particular body happens to be mine; primary reflection has to recall the facts that this body has just the same properties, that it is liable to suffer the same disorders that it is fated in the end to undergo the same destruction, as any other body whatsoever. Objectively speaking, it is non-privileged; and yet spontaneously, naively, I do have a tendency to delude myself about it, and to attribute to it – in relation to this malady or that – a sort of mysterious immunity; sad experience, however, in most cases dissipates such an illusion, and primary reflection forces me to acknowledge that the facts must be as I have stated them.

Let it be clearly understood that secondary reflection does not set out flatly to give the lie to these propositions; it manifests itself rather by a refusal to treat primary reflection's separation of this body, considered as just a body, a sample body, some body or other, from the self that I am, as final. Its fulcrum, or its springboard, is just that massive, indistinct sense of one's total existence which a short time ago we were trying, not exactly to define (for, as the condition which makes the defining activity possible, it seems to be prior to all definition) but to give a name to and evoke, to locate as an existential center.

It is easy to see that the dualism of body and soul, as it is postulated, for instance, in the Cartesian philosophy, springs from primary reflection, though in one peculiarly obscure passage, indeed, Descartes was led into talking of the union of body and soul as a third substance; but what I propose to do here is not, in fact, to comment on such well-known philosophical doctrines, but to get directly to grips with that non-transparent datum, which is constituted by my body felt as *my* body, before primary reflection has performed its task of dissociating the notion of body from the notion of what is intimately mine. But how will secondary reflection proceed in this case? It can only, it might seem, get to work on the processes to which primary reflection has itself had recourse; seeking, as it were, to restore a semblance of unity to the elements which primary reflection has first severed. However, even when engaged in this attempt at unification, the reflective process would in reality still remain at the primary stage, since it would remain a prisoner in the hands of the very oppositions which it, itself, had in the first instance postulated, instead of calling the ultimate validity of these oppositions into question. [MBI, pp. 91–93]

*   *   *

While we were walking yesterday on the hills above Mentone, I thought once more about the mastery of our own mastery, which is obviously parallel to reflection in the second degree. It is clear that this second mastery is not of the technical order and can only be the perquisite of some people. In reality, thought in general is what "one" thinks. The "one" is the technical man, in the same way as he is the subject of epistemology, when that science is considering knowledge as a technic. This is, I think, the case with Kant. The subject of metaphysical reflection, on the contrary, is essentially opposed to "one": this subject is essentially not the man in the street. Any epistemology which claims to be founded on thought-in-general is leading to the glorification of technics and of the man in the street (a democratization of knowledge which *really ruins it*). Furthermore, it must not be forgotten that technics stand on a lower step than the creation which they presuppose – a creation which itself also transcends the level where the man in the street holds sway. The "one" is also a step down; but by admitting him we create him. We live in a world where this man of straw begins to look more and more like a real figure.

. . . We must say that mystery is a problem that encroaches upon the intrinsic conditions of its own possibility (and not upon its data). Freedom is the basic example.

How can something which cannot be reduced to a problem be actually thought? In so far as I treat the act of thinking as a way of looking, this question would admit of no solution. Something which cannot be reduced to a problem cannot be looked at or treated as an object, and that by definition. But this representation of thought is in fact inadequate: we must manage to make abstraction from it. We must recognize, however, that this is extremely difficult. As I see it, the act of thinking cannot be represented and must be grasped as such. And what is more, it must apprehend every representation of itself as essentially inadequate. The contradiction implied in the fact of thinking of a mystery falls to the ground of itself when we cease to cling to an objectified and misleading picture of thought. [BH, pp. 125–126]

5. Mystery and Problem

The phrase "mystery of being, ontological mystery" as against "problem of being, ontological problem" has suddenly come to me in these last few days. It has enlightened me.

Metaphysical thought – reflection trained on mystery.

But it is an essential part of a mystery that it should be acknowledged; metaphysical reflection presupposes this acknowledgment, which is outside its own sphere.

Distinguish between the Mysterious and the Problematic. A problem is something met with which bars my passage. It is before me in its entirety. A mystery, on the other hand, is something in which I find myself caught up, and whose essence is therefore not to be before me in its entirety. It is as though in this province the distinction between in me and before me loses its meaning.

The Natural. The province of the Natural is the same as the province of the Problematic. We are tempted to turn mystery into problem.

The Mysterious and Ontological are identical. There is a mystery of knowledge which belongs to the ontological order (as Maritain saw) but the epistemologist does not know this, makes a point of ignoring it, and turns it into a problem.

A typical example: the "problem of evil." I treat evil as an accident befalling a certain mechanism which is the universe itself, but before which I suppose myself placed. Thereby I treat myself, not only as immune to the disease or weakness, but also as someone standing outside the universe and claiming to put it together (at least in thought) in its entirety.

. . . It follows from my definition of metaphysical thought as reflection trained upon mystery, that progress in this sort of thinking is not really conceivable. There is only progress in problematic thought. It is a proper character of problems, moreover, to be reduced to detail. Mystery, on the other hand, is something which cannot be reduced to detail. [BH, pp. 100–101]

*   *   *

Here we observe something basic to my whole thought, namely, that mystery is not, as it is for the agnostic, construed as a lacuna in our knowledge, as a void to be filled, but rather as a certain plenitude, and what is more, as the expression of a will, of an exigence that is so profound that it is not aware of itself and constantly betrays itself in forging false certainties; a completely illusory kind of knowledge in which the will cannot find any satisfaction, however, and which it destroys by an extension of the very *élan* it had yielded to in order to establish that knowledge in the first place. This appetite to know, this *Trieb zum Wissen* which is at the root of our greatness as well as of our misery, is transcended rather than satisfied in the apprehension of mystery. [CF, p. 152]

(**Note:** the concepts of problem and mystery, and their relation to Being, are also discussed in the next section on Being, in the second selection from *BH*—Editor)

*   *   *

6. On Being

The order of the problems seems to me to be as follows. Does our knowledge of particular things come to bear on the things themselves or on their Ideas? It is impossible not to adopt the realist solution. Hence we pass to the problem of Being in itself. A blindfold knowledge of Being in general is implied in all particular knowledge. But here, take care in what sense we use the words "Being in general." Obviously there is no question of Being emptied of its individual characteristics. I should express myself better if I said that since all knowledge concerns the thing and not the Idea of the thing – the Idea not being an object in itself and being incapable of conversion into an object except by a subsequent thought – process of doubtful validity – it implies that we are related to Being. The sense of these last words must be thoroughly explored.

The fact that I cannot possibly deny the principle of identity, except *in verbis*, at once prevents me from denying Being and also from holding an aloof attitude tantamount to admitting that "there may be Being, or again there may not." And, what is more, Being cannot by definition be put into the category of mere possibles. On the one hand, it is out of the question to think it contains a logical impossibility; on the other, we cannot treat it as an empirical possibility. Either there is not and cannot be experience of Being, or else this experience is in fact vouchsafed to us. But we cannot even conceive of a more privileged position than our own, in which we could *affirm* what our experience, as it now exists, does not let us affirm at present. Such a situation would be, at best, that of a being who *saw*, but was *ipso facto* beyond affirmation. The last refuge now possible for the opponent of ontology is to deny that an unconditional affirmation of Being is possible; in short, to take up his quarters in a relativist pluralism which asserts beings or lists of realities, but does not pronounce on their unity. But still, either words have no sense, or he is none the less implicitly asserting a unity which enwraps them. He will then have to take refuge in pure nominalism; that, I think, is the only cover left to him. He will have to deny that there is even an idea, much less a reality, corresponding to the word "Being." From this point of view, the principle of identity will be treated just as a "rule of the game of thought," and thought itself will be left radically separated from reality. From pure nominalism we slide into pure idealism. It is a dangerously slippery path, for idealism cannot reduce an idea to a symbol; it must see in it at least an act of the mind. And that introduces a new series of difficulties.

. . . I must honestly admit that under the persistent influence of idealism, I have been continually evading the ontological problem, properly so called. I have always, I admit, had the deepest reluctance to think according to the category of being: can I justify this reluctance to myself? I have really grave doubts of this. Pure agnosticism, i.e., a completely open mind about the affirmation of being, today appears to me untenable. On the other hand, I cannot take refuge in the notion that the category of being is in itself lacking in validity. Thought is betraying itself, and ignoring its own demands if it claims to substitute the order of value for the order of being, and at the same time is condemning itself to a state of most suspicious ambiguity in face of the given, even where it is its real business to grasp and define this given. On the other hand, can I maintain that the affirmation *"Being is,"* is despite appearances the mere formal enunciation of a "rule of the game" which thought must observe in order merely to work? To put it another way, is it a mere hypothetical inference equivalent to saying that if I assert a certain content, this assertion implies itself and consequently excludes those assertions which do not agree with it?

When I affirm that A is A, this means in idealist language that my thought, in asserting A, commits itself in a certain manner to an A-position; but this version does not really represent what I, in fact, think when I assume the identity of A with itself. This identity, for me, is really the condition of all possible structure (logical or real – this is not the place to take account of the distinction). We could not, in fact, deny the principle of identity without denying that thought can have a bearing on anything. We should be holding that, in proportion as I think anything, I cease to think because my thought becomes the slave of a content which inhibits or even annuls it. We could imagine a Heracleitanism or a hyper-Bergsonism which would go as far as that. Only the question would then be, whether this thought, which was not the thought of something, would still be a thought, or whether it would be lost in a sort of dream of itself. For my own part, I am convinced that the second alternative is the true one; and accordingly we may wonder whether I myself can think of myself (as thinking) without converting this "me" thought of, into something which is nothing, and which is thus a mere contradiction. But here I join forces with Thomism or at least with what I understand to be Thomism. Thought, far from being a relation with itself, is on the contrary essentially a self-transcendence. So the possibility of the realist definition of truth is implied in the very nature of thought. Thought turns towards the Other, it is the pursuit of the Other. The whole riddle is to discover whether this Other is Being. I must here note that it may be important to refrain from the use of the term "content," because of its idealist overtones. It is abundantly clear to me that access to objectivity, in the sense in which it is a stumbling block to a certain type of mind, must either be posited from the beginning or remain forever unattainable.

. . . I do really assert that thought is made for being as the eye is made for light (a Thomist formula). But this is a dangerous way of talking, as it forces us to ask whether thought itself is. Here an act of thought reflecting on itself may help us. I think, therefore, being is, since my thought demands being; it does not contain it analytically, but refers to it. It is very difficult to get past this stage. There is a sense in which I only think in so far as I am *not* (Valery?), that is, there is a kind of space between me and being. But it is difficult to see just what this means. In any case, I do notice a close kinship between thought and desire. Clearly in the two cases "good" and "being" play equivalent parts. All thought transcends the immediate. The pure immediate excludes thought, as it also excludes desire. But this transcendence implies a magnetization, and even a teleology. [BH, pp. 28–38]

*   *   *

[The] the complete withdrawal from the problem of being which characterizes so many contemporary philosophical systems is in the last analysis an attitude which cannot be maintained. It can either be reduced to a kind of sitting on the fence, hardly defensible and generally due to laziness or timidity: or else – and this is what generally happens – it really comes down to a more or less explicit denial of Being, which disguises the refusal of a hearing to the essential needs of our being. Ours is a being whose concrete essence is to be in every way involved, and therefore to find itself at grips with a fate which it must not only undergo, but must also make its own by somehow re-creating it from within. The denial of Being could not really be the empirical demonstration of an absence or lack. We can only make the denial because we choose to make it, and we can therefore just as well choose not to make it.

It is also worth noticing that I who ask questions about Being do not in the first place know either *if* I am nor *a fortiori what* I am. I do not even clearly know the meaning of the question "what am I?" though I am obsessed by it. *So we see the problem of Being here encroaching upon its own data*, and being studied actually inside the subject who states it. In the process, it is denied (or transcended) as problem, and becomes metamorphosed to mystery.

In fact, it seems very likely that there is this essential difference between a problem and a mystery. A problem is something which I meet, which I find complete before me, but which I can therefore lay siege to and reduce. But a mystery is something in which I am myself involved, and it can therefore only be thought of as a sphere where the distinction between what is in me and what is before me loses its meaning and its initial validity. A genuine problem is subject to an appropriate technique by the exercise of which it is defined: whereas a mystery, by definition, transcends every conceivable technique. It is, no doubt, always possible (logically and psychologically) to degrade a mystery so as to turn it into a problem. But this is a fundamentally vicious proceeding, whose springs might perhaps be discovered in a kind of corruption of the intelligence. The problem of evil, as the philosophers have called it, supplies us with a particularly instructive example of this degradation.

Just because it is of the essence of mystery to be recognized or capable of recognition, it may also be ignored and actively denied. It then becomes reduced to something I have "heard talked about," but which I refuse as only being for other people; and that in virtue of an illusion which these "others" are deceived by, but which I myself claim to have detected.

We must carefully avoid all confusion between the mysterious and the unknowable. The unknowable is in fact only the limiting case of the problematic, which cannot be actualized without contradiction. The recognition of mystery, on the contrary, is an essentially positive act of the mind, the supremely positive act in virtue of which all positivity may perhaps be strictly defined. In this sphere everything seems to go on as if I found myself acting on an intuition which I possess without immediately knowing myself to possess it – an intuition which cannot be, strictly speaking, self-conscious and which can grasp itself only through the modes of experience in which its image is reflected, and which it lights up by being thus reflected in them. The essential metaphysical step would then consist in a reflection upon this reflection (in a reflection "squared"). By means of this, thought stretches out towards the recovery of an intuition which otherwise loses itself in proportion as it is exercised.

Recollection, the actual possibility of which may be regarded as the most revealing ontological index we possess, is the real place in whose center this recovery can be made.

The "problem of being," then, will only be the translation into inadequate language of a mystery which cannot be given except to a creature capable of recollection – a creature whose central characteristic is perhaps that he is not simply identical with his own life.

. . . It is not enough to say that we live in a world where betrayal is possible at every moment, in every degree, and in every form. It seems that the very constitution of our world recommends us, if it does not force us, to betrayal. The spectacle of death as exhibited by the world can, from one point of view, be regarded as a perpetual provocation to denial and to absolute desertion. It could also be added that space and time, regarded as paired modes of absence, tend, by throwing us back upon ourselves, to drive us into the beggarly instantaneity of pleasure. But it seems that at the same time, and correlatively, it is of the essence of despair, of betrayal, and even of death itself, that they can be refused and denied. If the word transcendence has a meaning, it means just this denial; or more exactly, this overpassing (*Uberwindung* rather than *Aufhebung*). For the essence of the world is perhaps betrayal, or, more accurately, there is not a single thing in the world about which we can be certain that its spell could hold against the attacks of a fearless critical reflection.

If this is so, the concrete approaches to the ontological mystery should not be sought in the scale of logical thought, the objective reference of which gives rise to a prior question. They should rather be sought in the elucidation of certain data which are spiritual in their own right, such as fidelity, hope and love, where we may see man at grips with the temptations of denial, introversion, and hard-heartedness. Here the pure metaphysician has no power to decide whether the principle of these temptations lies in man's very nature, in the intrinsic and invariable characteristics of that nature, or whether it lies rather in the corruption of that same nature as the result of a catastrophe which gave birth to history and was not merely an incident in history.

Perhaps on the ontological level it is fidelity which matters most. It is in fact the recognition – not a theoretical or verbal, but an actual recognition – of an ontological permanency; a permanency which endures and by reference to which we endure, a permanency which implies or demands a history, unlike the inert or formal permanency of a pure validity, a law for example. It is the perpetuation of a witness which could at any moment be wiped out or denied. It is an attestation which is creative as well as perpetual, and more creative in proportion as the ontological worth of what it attests is more outstanding.

An ontology with this orientation is plainly open to a revelation, which, however, it could not of course either demand or presuppose or absorb, or even absolutely speaking understand, but the acceptance of which it can in some degree prepare for. To tell the truth, this ontology may only be capable of development in fact on a ground previously prepared by revelation. But on reflection we can see that there is nothing to surprise us, still less to scandalize us, in this. A metaphysic can only grow up within a certain situation which stimulates it. And in the situation which is ours, the existence of a Christian datum is an essential factor. It surely behooves us to renounce, once for all, the naively rationalist idea that you can have a system of affirmation valid for thought in general, or for any consciousness whatsoever. Such thought as this is the subject of scientific knowledge, a subject which is an idea but nothing else. Whereas the ontological order can only be recognized personally by the whole of a being, involved in a drama which is his own, though it overflows him infinitely in all directions – a being to whom the strange power has been imparted of asserting or denying himself. He asserts himself in so far as he asserts Being and opens himself to it: or he denies himself by denying Being and thereby closing himself to It. In this dilemma lies the very essence of his freedom.

From this point of view, what becomes of the notion of proving the existence of God? We must obviously subject it to a careful revision. In my view, all proof refers to a certain datum, which is here the belief in God, whether in myself or in another. The proof can only consist in a secondary reflection of the type which I have defined; a reconstructive reflection grafted upon a critical reflection; a reflection which is a recovery, but only in so far as it remains the tributary of what I have called a blindfold intuition. It is clear that the apprehension of the ontological mystery as metaproblematic is the motive force of this recovery through reflection. But we must not fail to notice that it is a reflexive motion of the mind that is here in question, and not a heuristic process. The proof can only confirm for us what has really been given to us in another way.

What becomes of the notion of Divine attribute? This, on the level of philosophy, is much more obscure. At present I can only see ways of approach to the solution. And anyhow, there can only be a solution where there is a problem, and the phrase "the problem of God" is certainly contradictory and even sacrilegious. The metaproblematic is above all "the Peace which passeth all understanding," but this Peace is a living peace, and, as Mauriac wrote in *Le Noeud de Viperes*, a Peace which is somebody, a creative Peace. It seems to me that the infinity and the omnipotence of God can also only be established in the reflexive way. It is possible for us to understand that we cannot deny these attributes without falling back into the sphere of the problematic. This is tantamount to saying that the theology which philosophy leads us to is essentially negative theology. [BH, pp. 116–122]

*　　*　　*

. . . we cannot yet solve the difficult problem of discovering the relations between value and being. One thing now seems reasonably clear: being cannot, it is certain, be indifferent to value; it could only so be if one were to identify it as a crude datum considered as existing in its own right, and that we are not justified in doing; in fact we must resolutely reject the idea of the existence in its own right of such a crude datum. The datum can only be grasped – Rene Le Senne has seen this very clearly – as an obstacle against which something hurls itself, and this something is not included in the datum; it will be found to spring, rather, from desire or aspiration. It will be legitimate, then, to say in a certain sense that where there is an experience of being, it is always a direct contradiction of this consciousness of a divorce between the datum and the aspiration. I once wrote, "Being is the culmination of hope, the experience of being is its fulfillment." The retort may be made that there is room after all, even in the world of the purely functional, for fulfillment. But in what does it consist? Most often it consists in having got through a task which is nothing but a task, with which, that is to say, there can be no interior identification. Let us imagine that I have answered so many letters today, or that I have sent out so many circulars in my day's work. It is true that I have done my work, but it has not been very different from a ticket collector punching tickets, or even a machine making so many revolutions. The human machine, indeed, is conscious of itself as a machine, and to that extent it is more than a machine, but there is no more real creation with one than with the other. I may add, to keep the thread of my argument clear, that any functionalized activity is manifestly the lowest depth of degradation to which creative activity can descend; and I cannot stress too emphatically that the word "fulfillment" can take on a positive meaning only from the point of view of creation. Moreover, it is clear, as we have already suggested, that creation is not necessarily the creation of something outside the person who creates. To create is not, essentially, to produce. There can be production without creation, and there can be creation without any identifiable object remaining to bear witness to the creation. I think that we must all, in the course of our lives, have known beings who were essentially creators; by the radiance of charity and love shining from their being, they add a positive contribution to the invisible work which gives the human adventure the only meaning which can justify it. Only the blind may say with the suggestion of a sneer that they have produced nothing.

Even so, when we say that being is fulfillment, are we perhaps still entangled in an ambiguity? The formula does not seem likely to satisfy a mind which insists on strict accuracy. The question is whether fulfillment can be considered on its own, or whether on the contrary it is involved in the life of a consciousness which finds in fulfillment something to satisfy a profound requirement. There is no doubt that the latter is the correct alternative. But if we do look at fulfillment in this light, shall we not find that it corresponds to what is only a phase in a development, and that this development involves, in relation to the fulfillment, a something which is this side of it and a something which lies beyond it – a preparation, a growth, but also a dissolution? Such an idea, which is after all relativist, can hardly be entertained if we identify being and fullness. It would seem better to admit that what we have called fulfillment should be interpreted in this context as a mode of participation in . . . – it is extremely difficult to find a definite word to fill this gap; or rather, although we can always avoid it by using an abstract word, there is a danger that the abstraction will be simply a stopgap. What does seem to emerge is that the problem presents itself very differently according to whether we are or are not in the domain of the spiritual. It is only analogically true to say of a plant which blossoms or fruits that it participates in the reality, the strictly ineffable reality, to which our tortuous and troublesome inquiry is directed. Without going into the almost insoluble complications contained in the theological notion of analogy, we may perhaps be content to say that the fulfillment realized in the flower or the fruit, is such only for an appreciating consciousness which apprehends the flower as a flower and the fruit as a fruit. Here the intervention of the appreciating consciousness is necessary for the fulfillment to be recognized as such; but this fulfillment is interiorized as soon as we enter the domain of either personal or inter-personal intersubjectivity. Now, perhaps, we can better understand why ontology, as we saw before, demands for its definition the addition of the dimension of intersubjectivity to that of objective knowledge. We could, in fact, say that fulfillment as such is meaningless – if it is considered from the angle of an objective or descriptive knowledge. And so we meet again the mysterious dovetailing (or articulation – I should use the same word in French) of being and value which we noticed before. [MBII, pp. 44–46]

Chapter 3

The Human Person

In the first section, Marcel comments on our tendency today to treat human beings as merely objects for scientific study, but such a view is misguided, and always leads to the impoverishment of our inner lives. Applied science is directly opposed to the realm of pure religion, which opens us up to the realm of the transcendent, which is part of the human condition, a realm which science by definition cannot have access to.

Part 2 turns to the notion of the situation, which is central to Marcel's view of the human person. Marcel holds that the experience of embodiment ensures that I am a being-in-a-situation, and this means that my experience and knowledge of the world will be shaped by my situation. My situation determines the complex web of relations I find myself intimately involved with at any given moment of my existence; he illustrates this point in this selection by means of the Vermeer example. I am not a spectator of life – mine or anyone else's, nor am I a spectator of the world. I am rather involved in the various projects and practices which shape and define my life. This is part of my essential structure as a human being.

He turns to the notion of encounter, which cannot be expressed in physical terms, and makes the profound point that there is a scale of relationships that involve this type of encounter with other human beings. He introduces also the notion of creative development, and links it to the area of ethics. Creative development allows us to avoid ethical formalism, which means the abstract analysis of ethical rules and cases; he holds that an emphasis on openness and intersubjectivity will foster an ethical approach to other persons, and so lead us to avoid treating ethical situations as logical problems to be solved.

In Part 3, Marcel turns his attention to a phenomenological description of the nature of the human person. He points out that the person is first posited in opposition to the "one" where the "one" is regarded as impersonal and anonymous, and where the person is characterized by courage and openness, both of which involve intersubjectivity. It is very difficult to describe the person in practical terms, but, negatively, we can say that the person is not an essence. This means that it is not possible to give a definite description of the nature of the person, or identify the essential properties of personhood, without distorting it, yet he notes that this very point could be said to be part of its essence metaphysically! This is the paradox of the human person. This passage is another good illustration of Marcel's philosophical style, where he struggles to express what is essentially inexpressible; we see him exploring various alternatives and suggestions in the attempt to give us a sense of the matter, as he probes the issue with very profound insight.

In the next section, Marcel again uses a simple everyday example of the young man feeling out of place at a party as a way of illustrating concretely the experience of intersubjectivity; he also notes that like the notion of "encounter," described above, there is a graduated scale of intersubjective experiences. Intersubjectivity also involves an internal relation – where both parties are affected by the relationship, as opposed to an external relation, where only one party is affected. The next passage is a brief reflection on intersubjectivity and value, and in the last selection he considers what it means to treat a person as Thou.

*   *   *

1. Man as Object of Science, and the Impoverishment of the Inner Life

By "applied science" I mean, in a general way, any branch of learning which tends to guarantee to man the mastery of a definite object. And so any applied science can obviously be regarded as manipulation, as a way of handling or molding a given matter. (The matter itself may belong to the mind, as in the science of history or psychology.)

Several points here are worth considering. (1) A science can be defined by the various handles which its object offers it. But conversely, an object itself is only an object in virtue of the handles it offers us, and this is true upon the most elementary level, of simple external perception. For this reason there is a parallel between advance in science and advance in objectivity. An object is more of an object, more *exposed* if I may put it like that, when the sciences under which it falls are more numerous or more developed.

(2) An applied science is in its very nature perfectible. It can always be brought to a higher and higher point of accuracy and adjustment. I

would myself add that the inverse is also true, and that nowhere else but in the realm of applied science can we speak of perfectibility and progress in an absolutely strict sense. In this realm alone can perfection be measured, since it is equivalent to output.

(3) This last point is perhaps most important of all. We are becoming more and more aware that all power, in the human sense of the word, implies the use of applied science. The simple-minded optimism of the masses today is founded on this fact. No one could deny that the existence of aeroplanes and wireless sets seems to the vast majority of our contemporaries to be the proof or palpable gauge of progress.

But we should notice the reverse side too – the price paid for such victories. From the scientific point of view, the world in which we live is apt to look at one moment like a mere field for development, and at the next like a subjugated slave. Any newspaper article about a disaster is full of the implicit suggestion that the monster we thought we had tamed is breaking out and taking its revenge. This is the point where applied science links up with idealism. Man is treated now not as Mind but as technical power, and appears as the sole citadel of orderly arrangement in a world which is unworthy of him; a world which has not deserved him, and has to all appearance produced him quite haphazardly – or rather, he has wrenched himself out of it by a violent act of emancipation. That is the full meaning of the Prometheus myth. I dare say a great many technicians would shrug their shoulders to hear so strange a mythology laid at their door. But if they are simply technicians and nothing more, what can they do about it? Nothing. They can only immure themselves in the fortress of their own specialized knowledge, and refuse, in fact if not in words, to tackle the problem of unifying the world or reality. . . . The subject will himself be seen as the object of possible sciences. The sciences are distinct and multiple, joined by hardly definable connections. It naturally follows – and experience fully proves – that the sciences themselves are less effective *as* sciences in proportion as they come to bear on realms where these water-tight compartments can no longer hold. That is why the sciences of psychology and psychiatry at present show such disappointing results.

But now we are faced with an appalling and quite unavoidable problem. The subject who lies in his turn at the mercy (if I may so phrase it) of applied science cannot be a source of clarity or a center of radiation; on the contrary, he can only enjoy a reflected light, a light borrowed from objects, since the sciences to be applied to him will inevitably be constructed on the model of the sciences directed upon the external world. . . . We do find in fact that unusually high development of the applied sciences goes with great impoverishment of our inner lives. The lack of proportion between the apparatus at the disposal of humanity and the ends it is called upon to realize seems more and more outrageous. I am sure to be told that the individual in the scientific state tends to be subordinated to social ends which go far beyond him; but is this really so? We have often heard the sociological sophistry that the whole contains more than the sum of its parts. But the truth is that although it undoubtedly contains something other than they do, all the evidence seems to show that the difference falls on the debit side and is expressible by a minus sign. There is no reason why a society of dunces, whose individual ideal is the spasmodic jigging of the dance-hall or the thrill of the sentimental and sensational film, should be anything more than a dunce society. It is obviously the inferior or rudimentary qualities in these individuals which draw them together. There is the difference, by the way, between a society like this and a community like the Church; for there the individuals do not swarm together mechanically, but do form a whole which transcends them. Such a community, however, is only possible because its members have each of them managed to keep inviolate that inner citadel called the soul, to which all sciences as such are opposed. . . .

These criticisms bring us indirectly to the definition of an order which stands in sharp and complete contrast to the world of applied sciences. Pure religion, religion as distinct from magic and opposed to it, is the exact contrary of an applied science; for it constitutes a realm where the subject is confronted with something over which he can obtain no hold at all. If the word transcendence describes anything whatever, it must be this – the absolute, impassable gulf which opens between the soul and Being whenever Being refuses us a hold. No gesture is more significant than the joined hands of the believer, mutely witnessing that nothing can be done and nothing changed, and that he comes simply to give himself up. Whether the gesture is one of dedication or of worship. we can still say that the feeling behind it is the realization of the Holy, and that awe, love and fear all enter into it simultaneously. Notice that there is no question here of a passive state; to assert that would be to imply that the activity of the technician, as he takes, modifies or elaborates, is the only activity worthy of the name. [BH, pp. 183–187]

* * *

2. Being-in-a-Situation

There is not, and there cannot be, any global abstraction, any final high terrace to which we can climb by means of abstract thought, there to rest for ever; for our condition in this world does remain, in the last analysis, that of a wanderer, an itinerant being, who cannot come to absolute rest except by a fiction, a fiction which it is the duty of philosophic reflection to oppose with all its strength.

But let us notice also that our itinerant condition is in no sense separable from the given circumstances, from which in the case of each of us that condition borrows its special character; we have thus reached a point where we can lay it down that *to be in a situation* and *to be on the move* are modes of being that cannot be dissociated from each other; are, in fact, two complementary aspects of our condition.

I have been pondering over our present topic for a great many years. It was about two years before the first World War, that is, in the days when I was starting on the investigations that led to the writing of my first *Metaphysical Diary*, that I was first led to postulate what I then called the non-contingency of the empirically given. I was chiefly interested in raising a protesting voice against a then fashionable type of transcendentalism, but I was also ready to acknowledge, from that date onwards, that the non-contingency of the empirical could be affirmed only in a rather special sense . . . as it is affirmed, in fact, by the subject itself, in the process of creating itself *qua* subject. . . . The notion of an ordeal, or test, to which the self subjects itself in the state of ingatheredness has played an essential part in our argument. . . . That notion, however, should now enable us to grasp also in what sense a man's given circumstances, when he becomes inwardly aware of them, can become, in the strict sense of the term, *constitutive* of his new self. We shall be tempted, of course, and we must resist the temptation, to think of a man's given circumstances, or of the self's situation, as having a real, embodied, independent existence *outside* the self; and of course when we think of a man's situation in this falsely objective way it does become hard to see how it could ever become his inner ordeal. But, in fact, as Sartre, for instance, has very lucidly demonstrated, what we call our given circumstances come into our lives only in connection with a free activity of ours to which they constitute either an encouragement or an obstacle. These remarks about circumstances should be linked up with my . . . remarks . . . about facts . . . about the reverberatory power of facts, as I might speak about the reverberatory power of circumstances; but . . . *in themselves* facts have no authority, and I might even have said no autonomous validity, and I might say the same thing now about circumstances.

There does, however, seem to be a very strict connection, if not even a kind of identity, between what I called earlier an *inwardness* and the non-contingency of given circumstances. In fact, we might say that we can hardly talk about inwardness except in the case where a given circumstance has positively fostered inwardness, has helped on some growth of the creative spirit. An artistic example might clarify things here. An artist like Vermeer, we might say, did not paint his *View of Delft* just as he would have painted some other view, if he had lived somewhere else; rather, if he had lived somewhere else, though he might still have been an artist, he would not have been Vermeer. He was Vermeer in so far as the *View of Delft* was something he had to paint; do not let us say, however, "He was Vermeer *because* he painted the *View of Delft*" for the conjunction "because," in its causal sense, has no bearing at all on the matter. Nothing at our present level of discourse can allow itself to be reduced to a mere relationship of cause and effect. If for Vermeer the view of Delft had been a mere spectacle, if he himself could have been reduced to the condition of a mere spectator, he would never have been able to paint his picture; let us even assert that he would not have been an artist at all. . . . And in my own case, I who am neither painter nor photographer am still something more than a mere spectator, in so far as I am capable of *admiring* the spectacle that I am contemplating. Do not let us ever forget, indeed, that to admire is already, in a certain degree, to create, since to admire is to be receptive in an active, alert manner. . .

It is from a similar point of view that we must treat the notion of an *encounter*, a notion whose importance has apparently not, at least until our own time, been clearly recognized by philosophers. As long as we keep our argument at the level of the *thing*, of the physical object, the encounter or collision of two objects can obviously be considered only as the fortuitous intersection of two series, of which one at least must be dynamic. A car bumps into a bus or into the side of a house. Their paths, as we say, crossed. But at this point we may be tempted to forget that, though there can be a collision between two objects, there cannot be an encounter or a meeting in the fullest sense of the word except between beings endowed with a certain inwardness: and the encounter between such beings resists, of its very nature, the attempt to express it in merely visual terms, where the collision of billiard or croquet balls, for instance, obviously does not. It is also clear that, at the level of the strictly human encounter, there is a whole scale of possible meetings that ranges from the quite trivial to the extremely significant. The nearer I get to the lower end of the scale, that is to say to a basic triviality, the nearer I get to an encounter that can be treated as an objective intersection of paths; humanly speaking it is nothing but a kind of elbowing. Every day in the street or the tube I elbow my way through hundreds of other people, and this elbowing is not experienced in any real sense as an encounter. All these unknown people present themselves to us, in fact, as mere bodies occupying a certain share of space in the *lebensraum* in which we have to maintain our own share of space and through which we have to thrust our way. But it is enough for some small thing to happen, something which is objectively speaking nothing at all, for us to transcend this subhuman level: for instance because of something about the tone of voice in which someone in the crush says, "I beg your pardon," or perhaps because of something about the smile accompanying such a simple phrase, there is a sudden spurt of clarity, of a clarity that has nothing in common with that of the intellect, but that can somehow light up, as a flash of lightning would, the obscurity – which is to say, fundamentally, the solitude – through which we are groping our way. Let us suppose now that two or three days later we encounter again "by chance," in the house of some third person, or in a hotel, the person whose smile lighted up our way for us; we find something very significant in this fresh meeting; and if somebody says to us contemptuously that it is a mere coincidence, we shall have a very distinct feeling, though not one that we can justify, that the person who expresses himself in this way has never reached the level of a human reality that cannot be reduced to the elementary schema of statics and dynamics that applies certainly well enough to physical objects in whose repeated collisions (if they were to collide several times) there certainly could be nothing but coincidence. This does not mean that we are acknowledging my right to explain this second meeting in, as it were, a mythological fashion, but only that the meeting takes place at the level of inwardness, that is to say, of *creative development*.

At this point in our argument, indeed, it should be obvious that as soon as there is life, there is also creative development. Or rather, to express the notion as I have expressed it already, in a vocabulary which is also that of Karl Jaspers, there is creative development as soon as there is *being in a situation;* and, of course, for our purposes, the term *life* does need to be defined in this way, phenomenologically, and without any reference to the data of biology. It may be that these rather simple remarks have a real relevance to ethics, and that they enable us to safeguard the idea of man's personal dignity without having recourse to that ethical formalism, which

is so often sterilizing in its actual effect on conduct, and which is too apt
to disregard the element of the irreducible in human situations and acts.
It should be added that in placing creativity at the basis of ethics, we at
the same time transcend that sort of ethical individualism for which the
individual tends to be thought of as something self-contained, a monad;
while on the other hand the direction of growth of our ethics would be
towards that open community of which what I have called the ideal city
is only the anticipatory skeletal form, the abstract ground-plan. [MBI,
pp. 133–139]

*   *   *

3. The Human Person

I want to proceed here as I did in connection with the act, i.e., by means
of concrete approaches which are as specific as possible.

It seems to me at least, that we cannot succeed in positing the person
by starting with the notion of something opposed to the individual (I
have not mentioned the word "define," for the task of defining raises
perhaps insurmountable difficulties). To a certain extent I find it equally
repugnant to consider it in terms of the opposition between person and
thing, although we shall certainly encounter this opposition again in
the course of our discussion and will have to justify it. I believe that
the person is first posited in opposition to the *man*, the *one*. Further, we
should observe that the one itself is not definable, strictly speaking. Yet
its distinctive characteristics are self-evident. In the first place, it is by
definition anonymous, without a face. In a way it cannot be apprehended;
I have no direct hold on it, it escapes me, it is by nature irresponsible.
In a certain sense, it is the very contrary of an agent. Its nature – does it
possess a nature? – has something self-contradictory about it, like that
of a phantom. It affirms itself as an absolute and is the very opposite of
an absolute. There is nothing more dangerous and yet more difficult to
avoid than our confusing it with impersonal thought. Actually, the *one*
is a thought that has regressed, a non-thought, the shadow of a thought.
But I perceive that this phantom is on the horizon of my awareness and
clouds it; it hems me in, it threatens to hem me in on all sides (I shall not
lay too much stress on such an obvious point, particularly in a world like
our own which is contaminated by the press). Further, reflection shows
me that the *one* is not only all around me; it is insufficient to say that it
surrounds me; it penetrates into me, it expresses itself in me; I spend my
time mirroring it. Most of the time my opinions are only a reproduction

of this *one* by an *I* which does not even know that it is reproducing it. To the extent that I reflect the opinions of my newspaper without even realizing that it is my newspaper I am reflecting, I participate in the *one*, I retail it, I market it (this is expressed by naive phrases like "everybody knows," "it cannot be doubted," etc.).

The mind here conjures up a pseudo-problem. How can we find room for the person between the surrounding one and the one which is penetrated? How can we localize it? If the problem is presented in these terms, it has no solution and is devoid of meaning. Any pretension to localize the person somehow rests on a confusion. The fact itself is evident although its acceptance raises serious difficulties.

What characterizes the person as opposed to the *one* which is anonymous, incapable of being apprehended, irresponsible?

We can start at the very heart of the question and affirm that to *confront* is what is characteristic of the person. We can maintain, from this point of view, that courage is the dominant virtue of the person – while the *one* seems on the contrary to be the locus of every flight and every evasion. Nothing is more typical in this respect than the mental procedure of someone who, not daring to adopt a position, hides behind this kind of shield: one claims that . . . one guarantees that. . . . Anyone who talks in this manner does not even identify himself with this *one*, but literally hides himself behind it.

It does not suffice to say that the person confronts the *one*; in the very fact of confronting it, he destroys it; to someone who tells me: "It has been claimed that the King of Belgium killed himself," I reply or should reply: "Who claims that?" The question, shifted to the plane of the *who*, exists outside of the realm of the *one*; by confronting the enemy, I force him to declare himself; the *one* is *qua* one, what never declares itself. But what does "declare itself" mean in this context? It means to specify itself. In this sense the person is an active negation of the *one*; I cannot acknowledge the *one*, i.e., ascribe the simplest rudiments of positivity to it, without becoming its accomplice, i.e., without introducing it into myself.

We must now analyze the act of confronting itself and consider its implications: some of these are intellectual. To confront is in a sense to envisage. What does one envisage? Primarily and essentially a situation. It is appropriate at this point to define as clearly as possible the nature of those intellectual operations whereby we grasp and master a situation. It seems clear that the simple fact of envisaging a situation instead of merely undergoing it – i.e., in short, incidentally apprehending certain aspects of it – already implies the kind of inner development which becomes prolonged into the act of confronting; but this still implies too much of a distinction and separation. In some respects, to envisage is already to confront.

This conclusion, however, must be developed in at least two directions. First, it is plain that to envisage is, in more than one sense, to *evaluate*. Here again, I believe, we must return to the situation.

First of all, a situation is in its very essence something which is not altogether clear; because of the fact that we exist in time, we are required to live in the non-resolvable. Hence there is a certain indeterminateness. And here the traditional problem of knowing whether this indeterminateness is or is not real loses any interest it may have. This indeterminateness exists, is even the essential datum for the consciousness which envisages and confronts. It therefore forces me to reckon together chances, probabilities, risks – which already involve an elementary form of evaluation; on the other hand, it is eminently true that to envisage a situation is at the same time to appraise it. Without a preliminary appraisal, I cannot confront. For to confront is to expose myself, i.e., to orient myself in a certain way, in a determinate direction, and only an appraisal can fix this direction.

. . . we can now understand the true meaning of the distinction between the individual and the person. It can be readily said that the individual *is the one in the fragmented state.* The individual is only a statistical factor – and conversely, a statistic is a possibility only on the level of the *one.* It may also be said that the individual is without a visage, without eyes. It is a specimen, a scrap.

In the second place, by characterizing the person in this way, we can catch a glimpse of what the absolute person might be, without, however, being able in any way to determine whether or not this is anything more than a metaphysical fiction. For the absolute person, the already fragile distinction between the relatively passive act of confronting and the active one of assuming is completely abolished; the absolute person tends to posit itself as wholly responsible for history. The *one,* diffused around it and absorbed within it, disappears in the complete specificity of its glance.

Yet I find it impossible to end this account with such a complete congruency, such a metaphysical apotheosis. I have to acknowledge that while the analyses whose outlines I have sketched seem to me completely accurate, I still have the impression that it is extremely dangerous to pretend to extract from them the elements of a positive philosophy. To expose my reasons for this, I believe, on the one hand, that the person is not and cannot be an essence, and on the other hand, that any metaphysics which is somehow established apart from, or protected from essences, is in danger of collapsing like a house of cards. I want only to mention this fact, because it really is something of a shock and disappointment to me. However, if we take up again at this time the problem of the relations between the individual and the person, I am afraid that we shall witness the resurgence of almost insurmountable difficulties.

. . . Two diametrically opposed metaphysical conclusions are entailed by the above, according to where we are inclined to center the idea of the person.

On the one hand, we can ask whether the idea of the person is not to a certain extent a fiction. Possibly there is no human person in the strongest sense of the term "person," nor can there be any; thus the person can become a reality only in God. For the rest of us, the person is perhaps but a point of view which is always in danger of degenerating into an attitude or into a palpitating anticipation, an appearance which can be degraded at any moment, can harden into a disguise, or can by some unholy masquerade, become a parody of itself.

Philosophical thought, however, can take another direction. Indeed, it can instead be maintained that the person is correlative with that anonymous or disguised factor which it confronts to the very end, and that in God, in whom this factor disappears, the person is abolished, simply because it is here that it fully emerges into the light.

It would be worthwhile to examine closely these two alternatives and to ask whether the opposition here between the two is not more verbal than real.

It should be noted that the most dangerous complications are introduced into the problem of the person because we perhaps have a tendency to confuse person and personality, on the one hand, and act and creation, on the other.

I simply wish to point out here that if we construe the personality as a stamp, as an individual imprint, as *Pragung*, it would not seem that a direct relation has necessarily been established between the personality in this sense and the person in the sense I have tried not so much to define as to evoke. Of course, we can argue here over the use of terms, but what is important to my mind is to understand that we are presented here with two aspects or two completely distinct levels of thought. The personality insofar as it is *Pragung*, is inwardness; it is given to us if not immediately, at any rate through certain media which are as mysteriously transparent as the voice or the glance – whereas in the act where it seemed that the person was focused, we can say that abstraction has been made of any kind of inwardness, of any rootedness. In these circumstances, however, is there not a danger that a philosophy based on the person rather than on the personality will almost ineluctably tend towards formalism?

Now in this connection we have the expedient of recalling the fact that the person, as I have said, confronts his past. Next, we can try to maintain that what is involved is the personality assuming itself, inwardness receiving its consecration from itself. However, it is not altogether certain that this solution is intelligible, and in any case, it would be impossible to remove the qualifications attached to this conclusion, for we know quite well that there are cases in which the person only succeeds in affirming himself by a kind of *coup d'état* whereby he strangles whatever inwardness exists within him. [CF, pp. 110–118]

*   *   *

4. On Intersubjectivity

The obvious example to take at this point is, of course, that of the shy young man who is making his first appearance at some fashionable dance or cocktail party. Such a young man is, as you so admirably express it in English, to the highest degree *self-conscious*. He feels himself the cynosure, and the extremely vulnerable cynosure, of neighboring eyes. It seems to him that all the other people at the party, none of whom he knows, are looking at him, and looking at him, too, with what meaningful glances! Obviously they are making fun of him, perhaps of his new dinner jacket which does not fit him as well as it should, perhaps of his black bow tie, which was all right when he last looked in the mirror, but now, he feels quite sure, has gone lopsided. And then, of course, he cut himself when he was shaving. And everybody must have noticed how clumsily he held his glass just a moment ago, so that some of the sherry slopped over. And so on, and so on. . . . To such a young man it seems that he has been literally thrown (as Christians were thrown to the lions) to the malevolent lucidity of other people's glances. Thus he is at once preoccupied with himself to the highest possible degree and hypnotized at the same time to a quite supreme degree by others, by what he imagines other people may think of him. It is this paradoxical tension which your excellent word *self-consciousness* so compactly expresses.

But on the other hand this tension is quite at the opposite pole from what I have at various times called, and shall here call again, intersubjectivity. And the opposite nature of the two things cannot be too heavily underlined.

Let us suppose that some unknown person comes up at our party to say a word or two to the shy young man and put him at his ease. The latter, to begin with, does not find himself entering into the direct relation with his new acquaintance that is expressed by the pronoun *you* but instead thinks of him as *him*. Why is *he* talking to me? What is *he* after? Is he trying to satisfy some sinister and mocking curiosity? Let us be on our guard anyway. Let us be extremely non-committal in our answers to his questions. Thus, because he is on the defensive with this other guest, our young man has to the least possible degree what can be described as a genuine encounter or conversation *with* him. He is not really *with* the other any more than he can help being. But in a very general fashion, indeed, one might say that it is the relationship expressed by the preposition *with* that is eminently intersubjective. The relationship that *with* expresses, here, does not for instance really apply to the world of objects, which, taken as a whole, is a world merely of juxtaposition. A chair is *alongside* a table, or *beside* it, or we put the chair *by* the table, but the chair is never really *with* the table in this sense.

But let us get back to our example and let us suppose that the ice is after all broken, and that the conversation takes on a more intimate character. "I am glad to meet you," says the stranger, "I once knew your parents," and all at once a bond is created and, what especially matters, there is a relaxation of tension. The attention of the young man ceases to be concentrated on himself, it is as if something gripped tight together inside him were able to loosen up. He is lifted out of that stifling here-and-nowness in which, if I may be allowed a homely comparison, his ego was sticking to him as an adhesive plaster sticks to a small cut. He is lifted right out of the here and now, and, what is very strange surely, this unknown person whom he has just met accompanies him on this sort of magic voyage. They are together in what we must call an elsewhere, an elsewhere, however, which has a mysteriously intimate character. Let us say, if you like, that they are linked to each other by a shared secret. I shall have to come back, no doubt, to the notion of the secret as a mainspring of intersubjectivity, but let us notice, before we leave our example, that ties of quite a different nature might have grown up between the stranger and the shy young man. A man whom I run into quite casually learns that I am very fond of coffee; coffee is desperately scarce in France at the time, so he gives me a hint about how to get some on the black market. One cannot say that this incident is enough in itself to create a bond between me and him; all we have in common is a *taste*, and that is not enough to draw us together at the ontological level, that is *qua* beings. And neither, on the other hand, is a taste for coffee, even combined with a certain broadmindedness about means of getting hold of coffee, enough in itself to create the sense of complicity and freemasonry in vice that might arise from the avowal, to somebody who shared it, of some much more dubious inclination. But such a sense of complicity is not really what we have in mind, either; rather it is in the sort of case where I discover that a stranger has recognized the deep, individual quality of somebody whom I myself have tenderly loved and who retains a place in my heart, that true intersubjectivity arises.

We could also take examples of intersubjectivity from artistic and religious experience. But it is clear that there would be no absolute discontinuity between the examples taken from ordinary life and those from the higher reaches of the spirit; on the contrary there would be a kind of graduated scale, with something like the mystical communion of souls in worship at the top end, and with something like an *ad hoc* association for some strictly practical and rigidly defined purpose at the bottom. But it would be possible to show that a single human relationship can work its way all the way up and down this scale; this, for instance, is quite obviously true of marriage. There may be moments of drought in marriage when the wife becomes for her husband merely that "silly creature who should have been busy darning socks, but there she was clucking round the tea table with a lot of old hens," and there may be almost mystical moments when the wife is acknowledged and loved as the bearer of a unique value to which eternal bliss has been promised. One might therefore say that there is an hierarchy of choices, or rather of invocations, ranging from the call upon another which is like ringing a bell for a servant to the quite other sort of call which is really like a kind of prayer. But, as I tried to show in my first *Metaphysical Journal*, in invocations of the first sort – where we press a bell or make some other sort of signal to show that we want service – the Thou we are invoking is really a He or a She or even an It treated pragmatically as a Thou. When I stop somebody in the street to ask my way, I do say to him, it is true, "Can *you* tell me how to get to such-and-such a Square?", but all the same I am making a convenience of him, I am treating him as if he were a signpost. No doubt, even in this limiting case, a touch of genuine intersubjectivity can break through, thanks to the magical powers of the tone of voice and the glance. If I have really lost my bearings, if it is late, if I fear that I may have to grope my way for hours through some labyrinthine and perhaps even dangerous warren of streets, I may have a fleeting but irresistible impression that the stranger I am appealing to is a brother eager to come to my aid. What happens is, in a word, that the stranger has started off by putting himself, as it were, ideally in my shoes. He has come within my reach as a person. It is no longer a mere matter of his showing me the way as a guide-book or a map might, but of his really giving a helping hand to somebody who is alone and in a bewildered state. This is nothing more than a sort of spark of spirituality, out as soon as it is in; the stranger and I part almost certainly never to see each other again, yet for a few minutes, as I trudge homewards, this man's unexpected cordiality makes me feel as if I had stepped out of a wintry day into a warm room.

On an occasion of such a sort, we have lingered for a moment on the threshold of intersubjectivity, that is, of the realm of existence to which the preposition *with* properly applies, as it does not properly apply, let me repeat, to the purely objective world. Within the realm of intersubjectivity, naturally, a whole throng of different sorts of relationships must be distinguished from each other. Words like "ensemble" in French, "together" in English, "zusammen" in German, can be entirely deceptive, particularly in the cases where they refer to traveling or even to working together, to the togetherness of the bus or the factory. There are certainly cases in which what is called collective labor can be considered, at least from the point of view of how it looks on the surface, as the arithmetical sum of the various special tasks performed by each separate individual. And yet even in such cases as this there is certainly also something that arithmetic cannot account for. There is at least in the background a sense of a common fate, there is certainly an indistinct awareness of the conditions to which all the workers in such a factory as we have in mind must without distinction subject themselves, finding, perhaps in every case, that such self-subjection goes against the grain. This feeling of community in effort and struggle that such factory workers have is quite enough in itself to deprive us of any right to treat them as simple units of force that can be added to each other. But we should recognize all the same that the level of reality represented by the preposition *with* can be a rather low and barren level – and this is naturally even more true in the case of the togetherness of passengers in a public vehicle. The content of this sort of reality, the reality for so many people of work and the journey to work, enriches itself only in the degree they learn to know themselves and to know their companions of bus or bench both in the uniqueness of their diverse beings and in the single color of their common fate. It is only on this condition that a true companionship can be created such as that, for example, which existed in the army during the late war between fighting soldiers, and perhaps in a greater degree still between prisoners-of-war and civilian deportees in various German camps. An ordeal endured in common is the cement of such companionships, it is what permits them to arise.

But when we talk of common sufferings cementing human *relationships*, let us notice that this word is likely to lead us into error, unless we take it in a much deeper sense than its usual one, for instance, in treatises on logic: we must think of the relationship between two terms as something that really does bind them, as something that causes them to negate themselves as simple, detached terms. We might make this point clearer if we said that relationships between things are external, relationships between people are internal. When I put the table *beside* the chair I do not make any difference to the table or the chair, and I can take one or the other away without making any difference; but my relationship *with* you makes a difference to both of us, and so does any interruption of the relationship make a difference. Between two people, in fact, who have an intimate relationship, a kind of unity tends to be created which makes a third person, who has not been initiated into the relationship, who does not participate in it, feel an intruder. [MBI, pp. 176–181]

*   *   *

However, we have here so vague, so superficial and especially so equivocal a determination. Is value conferred from without? Surely not; it can only be recognized imperfectly. It is therefore primarily experienced. It seems to me that it can only be incarnated first in order to radiate later. This is important because such a manner of thinking frees us immediately from the psychological aspect. Nevertheless one might insist: incarnated for whom? This question is, however, suspect. In asking it, one seems to set up a radical duality between the one who incarnates and the other from whom he incarnates. But everything changes if we affirm in principle a certain unity of a *we*, a radical non-isolation of the subject, including even the primacy of the intersubjective. For, from this point of view it is no longer a question of affirming something which would be first incarnated purely and simply, and another subject which would later, as it were from the outside, become aware of this incarnation. This is clearer still if we understand that the intersubjective is really within the subject himself, that each one is for himself a "we," that he can be himself only in being many, and that value is possible only on this condition. But perhaps it is necessary to postulate in principle that this interior or intersubjective plurality maintains the closest and least easily explorable relations with the extra-subjective plurality. My own are not only represented in me, they are in me, they are part of my very being (double falsity of monadism: I am neither *alone*, nor *one*). [P&I, pp. 200–201]

* * *

5. On the Nature of the Thou

People will say again, "But this distinction between the Thou and the He only applies to mental attitudes: it is phenomenological in the most exclusive sense of the word. Do you claim to give a metaphysical basis to this distinction, or a metaphysical validity to the Thou?"

The sense of the question is the really difficult thing to explain and elucidate. Let us try to state it more clearly, like this, for example. When I treat another as a Thou and no longer as a He, does this difference of treatment qualify me alone and my attitude to this other, or can I say that by treating him as a Thou I pierce more deeply into him and apprehend his being or his essence more directly?

Here again we must be careful. If by "piercing more deeply" or "apprehending his essence more directly," we mean reaching a more exact knowledge, a knowledge that is in some sense more objective, then we must certainly reply "No." In this respect, if we cling to a mode of objective definition, it will always be in our power to say that the Thou is an illusion. But notice that the term *essence* is itself extremely ambiguous; by essence we can understand either a nature or a freedom. It is perhaps of my essence *qua* freedom to be able to conform myself *or not* to my essence *qua* nature. *It may be of my essence to be able not to be what I am;* in plain words, to be able to betray myself. Essence *qua* nature is not what I reach in the Thou. In fact I treat the Thou as a He, I reduce the other to being only nature; an animated object which works in some ways and not in others. If, on the contrary, I treat the other as Thou, I treat him and apprehend him *qua* freedom. I apprehend him *qua* freedom because he *is* also freedom, and is not only nature. What is more, I help him, in a sense, to be freed, I collaborate with his freedom. The formula sounds paradoxical and self-contradictory, but love is always proving it true. On the other hand, he is really other *qua* freedom; in fact *qua* nature he appears to me identical with what I am myself *qua* nature. On this side, no doubt, and only on this side, I can work on him by suggestion (there is an alarming and frequent confusion between the workings of love and the workings of suggestion).

. . . The other, in so far as he is other, only exists for me in so far as I am open to him, in so far as he is a Thou. But I am only open to him in so far as I cease to form a circle with myself, inside which I somehow place the other, or rather his idea; for inside this circle the other becomes the idea of the other, and the idea of the other is no longer the other *qua* other, but the other *qua* related to me; and in this condition he is uprooted and taken to bits, or at least in process of being taken to bits. [BH, pp. 106–7]

Chapter 4

God and Religion

In our first section, we see Marcel's ambivalence toward proofs and arguments for God's existence, and more generally, toward attempts to show, in the manner of philosophy of religion at least, the rationality of belief in God, and of the religious worldview. He points out that those who are sincere believers do not need any arguments, and that rational arguments are not enough for those who do not believe. This shows, he suggests, that the affirmation of God is essentially an experience.

Religious experience partly involves an experience that our life is a gift to us. We have this experience because there is a spiritual side to human beings which is part of our nature, and it is the basis for the (rational) hope that our existence is ultimately meaningful. In this way, hope and faith go together, but it is a rational faith (and so rational considerations are relevant to the question of the existence of God). It is possible, nevertheless, to suppress our spiritual experiences, and this may be why rational arguments by themselves are not quite adequate. In addition, those who call for a conclusive proof of the existence of God are also making a mistake, because a proof cannot include the personal spiritual experience of the individual either giving or receiving the proof.

Some people are in denial about the realm of religious experience, and about their own spiritual side, but some are not, and are engaged in a genuine quest, and in that sense their experiences can be more authentic than those of some believers. Religious experiences ultimately require grace, and often emerge through intersubjective relations. Real religious faith requires a testimony, which I radiate to the other. This analysis takes us to the realm of mystery, Marcel explains. In these types of experience, I become a subject, rather than the subject being the point of departure.

The last selection of this first part is an example of Marcel doing philosophy of religion in the traditional way, because he takes us carefully through a rational discussion of some of the issues that arise in the atheistic argument that the existence of God is incompatible with the problem of evil. This is yet another indication that, despite his ambivalence toward this approach, he does engage in rational debate about religious matters, and thinks that such debate is necessary.

In Part 2, Marcel distinguishes between fidelity to a fellow human being and fidelity to God; the latter comes from the very depths of our being. The kind of belief affirmed in religious faith is always belief in a Thou, and this belief, which is really an experience, resists conceptual or philosophical analysis. Religious experience is founded on an experience of fidelity, an experience that involves recognition of an ontological permanency which transcends us and by which we endure – this experience is part of our human condition or situation. This part of the human situation Marcel refers to as the realm of Being, which overflows each person, and which again resists capture in conceptual knowledge. A believer, according to Marcel, has an unconditional hope, which is a response to the infinite Being, to whom we are conscious of owing everything. It is possible for us to reject these experiences, to refuse to recognize the realm of being, but this is to invite despair. However, the experience of the sacred in general is being lost in our contemporary world, yet it is difficult to suppress this realm completely because it is part of the nature of human beings.

Part 3 turns to Marcel's argument that in the order of faith there can be testimony only of the living God. The God of traditional theology or of philosophy is not a God to whom one can give testimony. He distinguishes between religion in general – and the experience of the transcendent that is part of the human condition – and its relationship to a particular historical religion, or how it might be experienced by an individual believer in a particular historical religion. In addition, in the experience of transcendence, freedom and grace must play a role – freedom because the individual as a practical matter is free to recognize or to refuse the experience of the transcendent, and grace because the experience comes to us from outside – but conceptual knowledge cannot fully express the nature of these experiences, and they cannot be made the subject of propositional knowledge. The philosopher must recognize this, and take it into account when attempting to think philosophically about religious belief. Philosophers must recognize that faith requires participation, and is fundamentally an experience founded on unconditional commitments, not an hypothesis. Another mistake we often fall into is to think of faith as being founded on a conditional commitment; it then becomes subject to doubt, temptation and rejection.

Marcel next turns to the subject of prayer. In this selection, he holds that authentic prayer involves a transcendence, which again is fundamentally an experienced relation, and so is not subject to the type of analysis that conceptual knowledge would recognize as valid. Authentic prayer involves uniting ourselves with God. We must appeal to secondary reflection to attempt to understand the real nature of prayer, because secondary reflection has an experiential aspect to it; it is a type of reflection that requires the personal experience of the inquirer, and so is most appropriate for thinking about the experience of prayer, unlike primary reflection which is the realm of conceptual knowledge, and which requires objective solutions that must be demonstrable in principle to anyone. At the root of the experience of prayer, Marcel suggests, is intersubjectivity – our relations, on a number of levels, with other human beings.

We conclude this selection on God and Religion with two short remarks by Marcel on creation, and on the disagreements between Catholics and Protestants.

*   *   *

1. On Proof, Atheism and Faith

We periodically witness the renewal of efforts to rehabilitate, to revamp, the traditional proofs of rational theology; I refer not only to neo-Thomism. . . .There is reason to think that at a certain level of philosophical reflection, it is just as impossible to declare the classical proofs adequate or completely adequate, as it is to reject them out of hand, the way we discard already postmarked stamps. The fact remains that certain distinguished minds found them adequate, and we cannot simply affirm that we are situated at a more advanced position than they on a road which is the high road of reason. Don't we have reason instead to assume that something essential is implied in their argument which cannot be completely expressed, something we try to explicate without being altogether confident that we can do so?. . . . Both reflection and history seem to point to the same fact, that the notion of a proof is inseparable from a prior affirmation, the truth of which one is later led to doubt, or rather, led to put in parentheses: we have to remove the parentheses. Proof is a phase of an inner eristic, and is always subordinate to an unvarying condition, or more precisely, to a system of values which cannot be questioned. Hence the less one acknowledges these values, or in other words, the weaker the spiritual tradition embodied in this system becomes – the more difficult it will be to produce a proof, just when the need for it becomes correspondingly pronounced. Thus we confront the paradox that generally, proof is efficacious only when we can if necessary do without it; while on the other hand, it will always seem circular to the person to whom it is directed and who must be persuaded. It must be repeated that we cannot substitute proof for belief; but what is more, there is a profound sense in which proof presupposes belief, in which it can only help to evoke an inner reaffirmation of the person who feels within himself a cleavage between his faith and what he takes to be a special requirement of his reason. [CF, pp. 177–179]

*   *   *

. . . it would be a serious mistake to interpret hope simply as an attitude that we have to take up; that would be as good as saying that we have to act as though we were hoping for all of us, the object of the hope being what one may call salvation. . . . Here it is that faith comes in; it is the presence of faith that gives to hope its intelligible frame. This makes it all the more important to emphasize that we are always open to the temptation of interpreting faith itself in a purely voluntarist sense. It is precisely at this point that we can appreciate the full value of the line of thought . . . concerning the bond between freedom and grace. Each one of us is in a position to recognize that his own essence is a *gift* – that it is not a *datum;* that he himself is a gift, and that he has no existence at all through himself. On the other hand, however, it is on the basis of that gift that freedom can grow or expand – that freedom which coincides with the trial in the course of which each man will have to make his own decision. This trial implies a decisive option. I can put my meaning to you by saying that the physical possibility of suicide which is engraved in our nature of incarnate beings is nothing but the expression of another much more profound and more hidden possibility, the possibility of a spiritual denial of self or, what comes to the same thing, of an impious and demoniac affirmation of self which amounts to a radical rejection of being. There is a sense in which that rejection is the final falsehood and absurdity; for it can exist only *through* someone who is; but as it becomes embodied it develops into perverted being.

It may perhaps be objected that if faith is understood in this sense, it does not seem to agree very closely with what is commonly meant by the word. The objector might ask me whether I have not systematically tried to shirk the fundamental question; that question will always be the existence of God. I am faced by two alternatives. Either I am in danger of reducing faith in God to an incommunicable psychic event, which implies the end of any sort of theology, and that means of all universality; or else I must try to find a way of framing something resembling a proof of the existence of God. The answer must be that everything we have said in the course of these lectures tends to show that this dilemma must be rejected – I should rather say transcended. It might well be that the idea of a proof, in the traditional sense of the word, of the existence of God implied a paralogism or a vicious circle. To assess this correctly, it would be necessary to proceed to an analysis of the phenomenological conditions of the act of proving. Proving always implies an "I undertake to . . . ." But this claim seems itself to be guaranteed not by the personal consciousness of a power, but by an essential unity which cannot but be apparent to a thought which has acquired for itself a certain degree of inner concentration. It is here that we can see the exemplary character of mathematical demonstration: whether or not it implies an intuition as its basis is immaterial; for even if that intuition exists, it is something quite other than a subjective datum. One fact, however, remains: the proofs that have been given of the existence of God have not always seemed convincing – far from it – even to the historians of philosophy who expounded them the most minutely. We might say briefly that when they spoke of "proofs" they put the word in inverted commas. We certainly cannot maintain that these historians failed to understand what they were saying. Should we, then, say that they had exposed a sophism which had escaped the notice of those who took the thought behind those proofs at its face value? That would be just as difficult to assert.

If the cosmological proof or the ontological proof "mean nothing" to a man – which implies that as far as he can see they do not get their teeth into reality, they skate on its surface – it may be that he is no further advanced on the high road of thought than those who are satisfied by them (I have in mind, briefly, the fact that the Kantian argument set up in the Transcendental Dialectic does not seem to have finally exploded the proofs). From another angle, however, I am no more inclined to think that those who wish to uphold the proofs can legitimately counter-attack by claiming that their opponents are guilty of a kind of fundamental ill-will which is basically pride. That is, indeed, too easy a method of discrediting one's opponent. In the first place this alleged ill-will calls for an effort of intelligent sympathy. We have reason to believe, as I have written before, that if the man against whom the charge is brought were to make his refusal fully explicit, he might say, "I refuse to follow this road, because *it leads where I do not want to go.*"

In one sense this is instructive, in another it is quite ambiguous. Why does the man not want to reach the affirmation of God which awaits him at the end of the journey? It may be because the affirmation seems to him incompatible with the fundamental data of experience, with the existence, for example, of suffering and all the forms which evil takes. A man like Albert Camus, for instance, cannot see how a God worthy of that name can tolerate the sufferings of children. But it may just as well be that in the atheist's eyes the affirmation of God would deaden the impulse that drives him, in his quality of free creature, to assert himself as an infinite in power; in that case, "where I do not want to go" would mean "I do not want God to be, because He cannot be without limiting me, that is, denying me." This explains the singular fact that what the "prover" puts forward as perfection is taken in an entirely opposite sense by his opponent; the latter takes it as an obstacle to the expansion of his own more or less divinized being, as a negation, that is, of the Sovereign Good. What is lacking here is the necessary minimum of agreement about ends, about the supreme value. But every proof presupposes, if it is to be given, at least this minimum of agreement. When that is lacking, the conditions in which proof is even possible are no longer present. The history of modern philosophy, as I said before, seems to supply abundant illustrations of the progressive replacement of *atheism*, in the grammatically primitive sense of the word, by an *anti-theism* whose mainspring is the will that God should not be. If, then, we consider the ineffectual character of the proofs of the existence of God, we cannot but notice again that deep split in the world of men. . . . So we stumble on this paradox: the proofs are ineffectual precisely when they would be most necessary, when, that is, it is a question of convincing an unbeliever; conversely, when belief is already present and when, accordingly, there is the minimum of agreement, then they seem to serve no useful purpose. If a man has experienced the presence of God, not only has he no need of proofs, he may even go so far as to consider the idea of a demonstration as a slur on what is for him a sacred evidence. Now, from the point of view of a philosophy of existence, it is this sort of testimony which is the central and irreducible datum. When, on the other hand, the presence of God is no longer – I shall not say felt, but recognized – then there is nothing which is not questionable, and when man models himself on Lucifer, that questioning degenerates into the negative will which I have already described. Can I hope to show this Lucifer-man his mistake? The truth seems to be that there is room for only one thing here, and that is a conversion which no creature can flatter himself he is capable of bringing about. There is hardly any phrase which is more detestable than "so and so has *made* so many conversions." It amounts to dragging conversion to the level of a piece of magic. Spiritually speaking such a comparison is outrageous. This, we have seen, is the domain of grace; it is also the domain of intersubjectivity, where all causal interpretations are a mistake.

All this is an illustration of the essentially paradoxical situation, in Kierkegaard's sense of the word, we find ourselves in when we are in the presence of God. Nothing we have said here can enable us to minimize its distressful and agonizing character; and yet it should by now be manifest that from the point of view I have adopted, anguish is not and cannot be the last word. I should be so bold as to say, on the contrary, that the last word must be with love and joy; and this I say from my innermost heart. If we want to satisfy ourselves of the truth of this, we must emphasize the intelligible aspect of faith; and in doing so, we shall be obliged to diverge very considerably from the views both of the Danish philosopher and even perhaps of the writer in whom we may well be inclined to see his precursor – I mean Pascal; for there is a connection which it is the philosopher's duty to underline with the utmost emphasis, the connection which binds together faith and the spirit of truth. Whenever a gap begins to open between these two, it is a proof either that faith is tending to degenerate into idolatry, or else that the spirit of truth is becoming arid and giving way to ratiocinative reason; and I think we have made it amply clear that this split is contrary to its nature, to its own proper impulse. [MBII, pp. 172–177]

*   *   *

Natural man is an historical reality and is defined with respect to an image of a universe changing in time; he is in history even when he tries to envision himself in a world conceived as alien to history, for this world still expresses his nature in its various forces and exigencies as these are realized in any given era . . . it is true that natural man not only evolves, since *homo naturalis* is also chiefly *homo historicus*, but that he can also disintegrate; I believe this disintegration in large measure explains . . . the reflective ineffectiveness on the apologetic level at least of so-called rational theology. . . . In the final analysis, it is because the unity of man has been shattered, because his world is broken, that we confront this scandal of proofs which are logically irrefutable but which in fact exhibit a lack of any persuasive power. [CF, p. 180]

*   *   *

I am a believer confronting a non-believer. And as I have indicated, I am sorely tempted to interpret this non-belief as implying bad faith or ill-will; we have also observed that I have to resist this temptation and open out to an understanding of the other such that I will be able to imagine this inner attitude as it is for him (and, not in terms of my own). For else I will be induced to think that something has been *given to me* which has not been given *to him;* further, I must reflect on the nature of this gift and of its counterpart. An examination of the conditions under which faith can be construed as a reality is appropriate here; I believe that this inquiry will help us to see that the word "reality" cannot be construed in this context either in terms of validity or practical efficacy. The question is rather one of discerning whether the believer – or rather whether I who claim to possess faith, have truly understood how to respond to the appeal addressed to me; such a response involves a testimony to which my life may or may not bear witness, a life construed not only in terms of specific, enumerable acts, or not mainly so, but in terms of what I give to, or radiate for, the other. In other words, the essence of real faith completely precludes assimilation to a possession of which I can avail myself; as soon as I claim this to be the case, faith is denatured; hence I am not led to judge the discrepancy between myself and the faith which I thought was my due, i.e., to take into account my non-belief which exists at the center of which I call my faith. A communication is immediately established, therefore, between me and the person who avows simply that he is a non-believer – a communication established in the light of truth which is also a light of charity; this communication can also eventuate in a transposition, which is not objective to be sure – for this is meaningless – affecting the relation I established between myself and the other; for I can arrive at the point of acknowledging that the other who avows he is a non-believer, bears witness more truly and more effectively than I who claim to be a believer, to the reality embodied in my faith. . . .

We can distinguish between problem and mystery in terms of the above complex train of reflections; for this reality to which I am open when I invoke it can in no way be identified with an objective datum the nature of which must be contemplated and cognitively determined. It may be said at once that this reality gives *me* to myself insofar as I give myself to it; it is through the mediation of the act in which I center myself on it, that I truly become a subject. I repeat, *that I become a subject*: the fatal error of a certain species of idealism really consists in a failure to see that being a subject is not a fact nor a point of departure, but a conquest and a goal. [CF, pp. 181–183]

*   *   *

Another thing: we know that the atheist claims to have made good a collection of facts, and that these facts are incompatible with the existence of God. All these facts are connected with the presence of evil in the world. But what then comes in as the factor that determines his position is not so much his actual experience of evil – believers, also have experienced evil in all its manifestations – as a judgment of absolute incompatibility. The atheist's opinion, accordingly, puts itself forward as resting on a rational basis. But it would be well to have a close look at this judgment of incompatibility, and in doing so I shall have to re-open my earlier analysis.

When I am speaking of a particular person and say, "If that person had been there, such a thing would not have happened; if it happened, it must be because that person was not there," my ground for so speaking is a precise knowledge, or my claim to a precise knowledge, of the person in question. A nurse would have stopped the child from playing with the matches; which means, that she is prudent and careful, she can be trusted completely; she could not have let the child play with matches. But two suppositions are implied in this: first, that the person – the nurse in this case – does really exist; and secondly, that we know her so well that we can say what sort of person she is and what she would do in any given circumstances. The atheist, however, relies not on an experience but on an idea, or pseudo-idea, of God: if God existed, He would have such and such characteristics; but if He had those characteristics He could not allow, etc. His judgment of incompatibility, in fact, is based on a judgment of implications. Or rather, what he wants to say is that if the word "God" has any meaning – of which, indeed, we cannot be certain – it can be applied only to a being who is both completely good and completely powerful. This part of the argument might well be granted; but not so with what follows. When I am speaking of the nurse, I am relying on situations or circumstances which actually occurred, and in which she effectively demonstrated her prudence; or at least on an inner certainty of what I should have done in her place. But does such an assertion retain any meaning when it is applied to the behavior of God? Whether those last words have any meaning at all and whether the idea of divine behavior is not self-contradictory, is a very serious question, but we can leave that on one side for the moment. If I proceed to draw conclusions from what the divine behavior has been in any particular historical instance, then I am *ipso facto* debarred from agreeing with what the atheist maintains. But is the alternative any better? Can I so put myself in the place of God as to be able to say how I should have behaved in any particular circumstances, what I should have allowed and what I should have forbidden? We may note that when we are speaking of an important public figure who is called upon to make a crucial decision, we often find it impossible to imagine ourselves in his place; in fact the very idea of doing so seems ridiculous. If we pursue that line of thought, we are obliged to recognize the absurdity of trying to put ourselves in God's place. It may be objected, of course, that the statesman has to grapple with a situation which is not of his making, though he has to disentangle it, master it and finally find a solution. But should not God, if He is thought of as a creator, be conceived as having the privilege of needing only to exercise His will? The atheist will say that, if He does not will good, it must be because He Himself does not exist. The extreme insecurity of this position is now very apparent to us, and later it will become progressively more clear that the affirmation of God cannot be separated from the existence of free beings who have reason to think of themselves as creatures. In these circumstances, or at least from one point of view – metaphysically speaking, it may not be a final one, but in the complicated pattern of human life we cannot overlook it – we have grounds for admitting that God Himself may have to take into account (it would be ridiculous to use the word "suffer"), in the very name of his creative intention, a state of affairs – an extraordinarily complex pattern, that is, of situations for which men have the right to hold themselves responsible. From this point of view the comparison between God and the statesman in whose place we cannot put ourselves, is not fundamentally as absurd as it seemed at first. This is rather an exoteric way of envisaging the relation between God and the finite beings which He has created free, and I do not claim that it is metaphysically satisfactory. It is only a halting place, and for the moment we may have to leave it behind. But, whatever happens, we cannot just rush by this halt, as an express rushes through a station at which it is not stopping. Let us put it another way, and say that though objections may be raised to the notion of something being *permitted by God,* permitted without being willed, yet it is a notion that cannot just be neglected. It provides a sort of resting place on a certain road; again it provides a way, rather a negative way, no doubt, of rejecting another much cruder conception of the relation between the divine will and the history of mankind. [MBII, pp. 72–75]

*   *   *

2. Fidelity, Hope, and God as "Absolute Thou"

. . . Fidelity to a specific individual who is given in our experience, seems to the person who *lives* it rather than who views it from the outside, as irreducible to that feeling linking consciousness with itself and its contents.

On the other hand, an absolute fidelity, which is therefore vowed not to a particular being, to a creature, but to God himself, is in danger of being construed today by the critical mind which is generally allied to the common sense view, as an unconscious egocentricism which ends up by hypostatizing a subjective datum.

In other words . . . it is readily granted that on the empirical level there can be a real fidelity with respect to a *thou* having an objective reality. The fact is, however . . . if I stay on the hither side of the ontological affirmation strictly speaking, I can usually call into question the reality of the bond linking me to some particular being; in this domain disappointment is always possible in principle, i.e., the separation of the idea from being; I can always be induced to recognize that it is not to this creature as she really is that I have been faithful, but to the idea I have conceived of her, an idea which experience has belied.

But on the other hand, the more my consciousness is centered on God himself, evoked – or invoked – in his real being, the less conceivable this disappointment will be; in any case, if it comes, it will be in my power to blame only myself for it, and to see in it only the sign of my own inadequacy.

Hence this ground of fidelity which necessarily seems precarious to us as soon as we commit ourselves to another who is unknown, seems on the other hand unshakable when it is based not, to be sure, on a distinct apprehension of God as someone other, but on a certain appeal delivered from the depths of my own insufficiency *ad summan altitudinem*; I have sometimes called this the absolute resort. This appeal presupposes a radical humility in the subject; a humility which is polarized by the very transcendence of the one it invokes. Here we are, as it were, at the juncture of the most stringent commitment and the most desperate expectation. It cannot be a matter of counting on oneself, on one's own resources, to cope with this unbounded commitment; but in the act in which I commit myself, I at the same time extend an infinite credit to Him to whom I did so; hope means nothing more than this.

. . . We are now concerned with determining how, beginning with that absolute fidelity which we may now call simply faith, the other fidelities become possible, how in faith and no doubt in it alone, these find their guarantee. . . .

. . . Belief in the strong sense of the term – not in the sense of believing that, i.e., assuming that – is always belief in a *thou*, i.e., in a reality, whether personal or supra-personal, which is able to be invoked, and which is as it were, situated beyond any judgment referring to an objective datum. [CF, pp. 166–167]

*   *   *

Perhaps on the ontological level it is fidelity which matters most. It is in fact the recognition – not a theoretical or verbal, but an actual recognition – of an ontological permanency; a permanency which endures and by reference to which we endure, a permanency which implies or demands a history, unlike the inert or formal permanency of a pure *validity*, a law for example. It is the perpetuation of a witness which could at any moment be wiped out or denied. It is an attestation which is creative as well as perpetual, and more creative in proportion as the ontological worth of what it attests is more outstanding.

An ontology with this orientation is plainly open to a revelation, which, however, it could not of course either demand or presuppose or absorb, or even absolutely speaking understand, but the acceptance of which it can in some degree prepare for. To tell the truth, this ontology *may* only be capable of development *in fact* on a ground previously prepared by revelation. But on reflection we can see that there is nothing to surprise us, still less to scandalize us, in this. A metaphysic can only grow up within a certain situation which stimulates it. And in the situation which is ours, the existence of a Christian datum is an essential factor. It surely behoves us to renounce, once for all, the naively rationalist idea that you can have a system of affirmation valid for thought *in general*, or for *any consciousness whatsoever*. Such thought as this is the subject of scientific knowledge, a subject which is an idea but nothing else. Whereas the ontological order can only be recognized personally by the whole of a being, involved in a drama which is his own, though it overflows him infinitely in all directions – a being to whom the strange power has been imparted of asserting or denying himself. He asserts himself in so far as he asserts Being and opens himself to it: or he denies himself by denying Being and thereby closing himself to It. In this dilemma lies the very essence of his freedom. [BH, pp. 120–121]

*   *   *

It really seems to be from this point of view that the distinction between believer and unbeliever stands out in its true meaning. The believer is he who will meet with no insurmountable obstacle on his way towards transcendence . . . insofar as I make my hope conditional I myself put up limits to the process by which I could triumph over all successive disappointments. Still more, I give a part of myself over to anguish; indeed I own implicitly that if my expectations are not fulfilled in some particular point, I shall have no possibility of escaping from the despair into which I must inevitably sink. We can, on the other hand, conceive, at least theoretically, of the inner disposition of one who, seeing no condition or limit and abandoning himself in absolute confidence, would thus transcend all possible disappointment and would experience a security of his being or in his being, which is contrary to the radical insecurity of Having.

This is what determines the ontological position of hope – absolute hope, inseparable from a faith which is likewise absolute, transcending all laying down of conditions, and for this very reason every kind of representation whatever it might be. The only possible source from which this absolute hope springs must once more be stressed. It appears as a response of the creature to the infinite Being to whom it is conscious of owing everything that it has and upon whom it cannot impose any condition whatsoever without scandal. From the moment that I abase myself in some sense before the absolute Thou who in his infinite condescension has brought me forth out of nothingness, it seems as though I forbid myself ever again to despair, or, more exactly, that I implicitly accept the possibility of despair as an indication of treason, so that I could not give way to it without pronouncing my own condemnation. Indeed, seen in this perspective, what is the meaning of despair if not a declaration that God has withdrawn himself from me? In addition to the fact that such an accusation is incompatible with the nature of the absolute Thou, it is to be observed that in advancing it I am unwarrantably attributing to myself a distinct reality which I do not possess. [HV, pp. 46–47]

*   *   *

Nevertheless, it seems to me that something in us protests in a more or less inarticulate fashion against this radical elimination of unconditional commitment. Should we say that we are dealing here simply with a case of a simple anachronism and that its sacred character is precisely what ought to be considered antiquated?

But here we are encountering a type of assertion which is becoming increasingly fashionable in our times and which we find it important to subject to rigorous examination. It consists in judging that for contemporary man such an unconditional way of being or of belief is no longer necessary. Even some theologians have not been exempt from contamination by this odd historicism; I am thinking in particular of the rationalism underlying, it seems to me, the thinking of Bultmann. "No man today," he says, "can believe any longer in a miracle."

Surely those who express such thoughts must be aware that in fact there exist men, perhaps even in great numbers, who do not seem to suspect any such incompatibility between their belief and the requirements, set up as normative, for modern man. But this fact could be met by treating that anachronistic mentality as a fossil – as if one were dealing with individuals who did not know they belonged to historical layers covered over by later sedimentations.

For my part, however, I would say that we should denounce right now the illusion associated with this type of assertion. . . . From what I have said there is every reason to view with the greatest distrust the presumption of those who dare to assert, for example, the disappearance of the sacred.

It is appropriate at this point to introduce an essential distinction: It is easy to see how in the world around us the process of abolishing the sacred is accomplished and is accelerated, and it is not difficult for us to imagine that here or there a state of things could be established so that the very meaning of the word sacred would no longer be understood by anyone. But this by no means signifies that, judged from the standpoint of reflective thought this obliteration *de facto* of the sacred corresponds to a refutation *de jure*. Everything seems to indicate that this radical profanation could not be accomplished without striking a blow at what are probably unformulated needs which are deeply inscribed in the very heart of a human being. [EBHD, pp. 72–74]

*   *   *

3. Testimony and Faith

One might, it is true, ask whether it is not possible to *testify* to an idea, that is to say to something which is in itself beyond time. This, however, would seem to be possible only in so far as the idea has been embodied, for example when justice has been violated in the person of the innocent victim of an unjust sentence; and thus we come back to a certain historical datum. To conduct an active campaign for the recognition of the innocence of the victim will be to act as a witness. We must, I think, emphasize that the same cannot be said of the philosopher or the moralist who writes a treatise on justice, unless by so doing he incurs the punishment which tyrants inflict on those who defy them. But here again we are back in the historic.

It is not difficult, I think, to proceed from all these rather elementary considerations to the important idea that in the order which matters to us – that of faith – there can be testimony only of the living God. The God with whom theologians of the traditional type are most frequently concerned, the God whose existence they claim to demonstrate to us, cannot for all that be the occasion of any testimony; and to that extent one might be tempted to say that He cannot concern the believer as such. That God, who is in fact the God whom Pascal calls the Philosophers' God, stands in a dimension which is not and cannot be that of faith. But, if we skip several stages, we are led to ask ourselves whether the living God is not inevitably a God who has become incarnate, and whether it is not to this same incarnation that the testimony is in the first place directed. *Grosso modo* we might put it concretely by saying that if belief in a living God is not to sink into mythology, it means, not exclusively but at least secondarily, that every approach to justice, for example, or to charity, in the person of my neighbor, is at the same time an approach to this God Himself; and this entails an entirely concrete but quite mysterious relation between this living God and this creature who is my neighbor. If this were not admitted, what one maintained to be a living God would thereby be reduced to an idea which is of necessity unalterable and against which I cannot sin. We may note that the introduction of the word "sin" is inevitable at this point, and moreover that it is clear that since the world of testimony is that of freedom, it is also one in which one can refuse to testify, or else in which one can be a false witness, etc., that is, a world in which there can be sin.

If we carry on this line of thought, we shall understand quite clearly that in the Christian scheme the witness is not only someone who has been a contemporary of Christ in the chronological meaning of the word, or a direct recipient of His teaching. The effect of Incarnation is in fact to spread radiance, and it is just for that reason that today there can still be witnesses of Christ, whose evidence has a value that is not only exemplary but strictly apologetic.

This is not, however, the place in which to develop these corollaries. What is more important is to understand that here we have the interlocking of an historical religion with what could only be religion in general or faith in general, and which is in fact only the priming of a concrete spirituality. But when I speak of interlocking, it must be realized that there can be no question here either of an analytical bond – that is self-evident – or even of any dialectical chain. The philosopher who appreciates the exigence of transcendence in its fullness, that is, who cannot rest satisfied either with what takes place in this world, or even with the world itself considered in its totality – a totality, moreover, which is always fictitious – may nevertheless fall short of conversion to any particular historical religion. In such a conversion there is no movement imposed by necessity, but it must be added that neither is there any free act in the meaning which the word consistently bears, at least if freedom is supposed to be a spontaneous initiative proceeding from myself. Conversion cannot but appear to a man who has not been converted as depending on conditions which are foreign to his will and even strictly impossible to foresee. There is a gap, and it is not man's business to fill it up for himself. Grace will appear before conversion as an incomprehensible power which may perhaps operate, but may also fail to intervene. Let us note that *at a distance*, if I may say so, grace inevitably appears as some sort of a cause; but this is connected with a misconception of grace. This is, moreover, bound up with the fact that an historical religion – and here we must think primarily of Christianity – almost inevitably appears as an object of scandal to one who is not yet a convert. All we can say is that at its furthest extension metaphysical thought perceives the possibility of conversion, but perceives it as being dependent on conditions which it is beyond the power of freedom to bring about by itself. We should certainly add, as a rider to what we said above, that conversion is the act by which man is called to become a witness. This presupposes, however, that something has actually happened in which he will have to discern the action of the living God, or again a recognizable call which he will have had to answer. Here we can put our finger precisely on the interlocking of freedom and grace, and we see how neither can in any way be thought of without the other. But we have reached the point where it must be clear at the same time that we should be making a mistake, were we to try to localize this conversion at a given moment of its duration. The fact or the occurrence to which we give the name conversion, is only the starting point of a movement which must progress without any break. The most serious error of which the converted can become guilty is that of believing that he is placed or installed once and for all in some privileged position from which he can look condescendingly on the tribulations of those who have not yet joined this sort of "home." It is just this idea of "home" which must be rejected with the utmost emphasis, at least if this "home" is conceived not as a goal, as something to be reached, but as being already dwelt in. The converted, in the only sense of the word we can accept, must realize that there is nothing on this plane which can be won once and for all, that there is a constant possibility of relapse, and that he is in danger of falling much lower even than his original starting-point; and this for the weighty reason that if he relapses he will no longer have the benefit of the sort of allowance that is made for the state of the honest unbeliever.

We may add that any interpretation of this in the language of possession would be radically mistaken. We could also draw certain conclusions from it about the attitude which those who are believers of long standing should adopt towards recent converts. Above all they should be careful not to treat them as recruits, whose enrolment provides them with reinforcements; and it is here that we might well bring out the extreme importance of a certain tact which is connected with the concrete respect or delicacy we have already had occasion to mention. This tact may be well compared, I think, to the precautions which a gardener has to take to ensure the growth of a very delicate plant. But in this case, by an extreme paradox, the gardener has to see himself as a plant exposed to the inclemency of time and habit. By a sort of remarkable inversion, he has to send himself back to the novitiate, so that the conditions under which the novice lives may give him immunity for a time from these inclemencies. Thus there comes about a completely spiritual interaction, which, in as much as it is a life and not just a disposition, has its roots in charity itself. From this point of view the philosopher seems to be better able to distinguish the nature of a *Church*. Ecclesiological reflection should take for its object the bringing to the surface of the implications of this change. It would doubtless allow to emerge, to be developed (as we use the word "develop" in photography) the existence of a concrete intelligible medium outside of which what we call faith is certainly in danger of being degraded into a rather erratic disposition, or even to an unguided phenomenon which to an external observer would keep a dangerously problematical character.

These are the chief considerations we should take as a starting point from which to try to clarify the conditions or guiding rules for the philosopher who wishes to direct his thought to faith. What is required of him is in the first place to take this question of faith seriously, or, if you like, to acknowledge its reality, even if in all honesty he cannot say that he personally adheres to this faith, and if for some reason ingrained in his nature, the idea of conversion is repellent to him.

We must, however, at this point, anticipate an objection which threatens the whole basis of our argument: what, then, is the value of this exigence to which the philosopher must bow? By what right do we claim that he must give faith the benefit of a favorable prejudice, instead of keeping a strictly neutral attitude towards it? The very use, however, of the expression "favorable prejudice" seems to be bound up with a misunderstanding which it is important to clear up; the phrase could only be justified if what we are concerned with were comparable to an hypothesis. Any hypothesis at all should in fact be considered by the philosopher with absolute impartiality. But we must put out of our mind the idea that we are dealing with anything comparable to an hypothesis, and it may well be useful to sum up briefly the reasons for rejection. We spoke of the possibility and even the necessity of a purification in such a sphere. But this implies a participation on the part of the subject which is quite inconceivable in the sphere of knowledge properly so called. Now, an hypothesis can never be anything but a preliminary stage on the road to knowledge. It is valueless except in so far as it is capable of being either confirmed or disproved by experience. We may add that in either case it will cease to exist as an hypothesis. In the case with which we are concerned, anything of this nature cannot be conceived; and to understand this, it is only necessary to recall the nature of the credit which I have opened in favor of the being I love. It would be absurd to say, "I admit as a plausible hypothesis that he will not deceive me." If I love him, I lay it down as an axiom that he *cannot* deceive me. It is possible, of course, that I may be mistaken and that I may come to realize my mistake, but this will make no real difference to the fact that I have had faith in this being, and in a sense which transcends every possible supposition. This becomes infinitely more clear when it is a question of the *transcendent Being*, to whom I am compelled to open an absolute, that is to say an unconditional, credit; and we should have no hesitation in saying that the more unconditional my faith is, the more genuine it will be. No doubt – and we cannot emphasize this too strongly – there will be no lack of circumstances which may make me falter; if the being whom I love best in all the world is taken from me in incredibly cruel or brutal circumstances, I shall be unable to refrain from protesting: "If there were a God. . ."; or, which comes to the same thing, "If He possessed the attributes with which we commonly endow Him, He would not have allowed this monstrous happening." But if I yield to this temptation, shall I not thereby reveal that my faith implied an unacknowledged condition? To be sincere, I shall have to realize that what I should have said in the first instance was, "I shall believe in You, God, in so far as You ensure for me the minimum of moral comfort I need, but not beyond that point." Then it will be as though I were conscious of having made some contract with God and as though I accused Him of having broken it. To look at it more deeply, it will be as though I said, "It looks as though this contract had been broken by the other party; what really happened, however, was that the other party did not exist, and I made my contract with an imaginary being; for if he had been real, he could not have brought himself to incur the guilt of such a crime."

Objectively speaking, there is nothing, indeed, which can prevent me from giving way to this sort of indignation, and here what we said about the relations between freedom and faith is brought out with great clarity. Each one of us, if he examines himself honestly, will have to confess that he is liable to take up such an attitude when overburdened by misfortune. The impulse will be the more irresistible, also, the more his relation to God has not been a living relation, but has been reduced to a collection of abstract theological statements. In such statements there is certainly nothing strong enough to resist the assault of concrete facts. But reflection, whenever it is positive, that is, recuperative, is bound to realize that a being in whom faith really resides will undoubtedly find, not in himself, indeed, not in his own unaided resources, but by the help of God's own presence, the strength to repel this temptation.

It is true that one could counter by saying, "So deep a faith can only be a gift of God. How can I be blamed if this gift has not been granted to me?" Again we find that the root of the objection lies in a materialist representation, the picture of some deficiency of supply. In fact, however – and here we face one of the central paradoxes we must particularly stress – if this way of picturing it makes me drive a wedge between my faith and myself which separates me from the thing whose possession is my ultimate aim, I am no longer really speaking about faith nor about grace; I am putting in their place pure fictions, instead of the mysterious and indivisible unity of freedom and grace. We must, of course, add that everything we have just said has a real foundation in – and is not simply confirmed by – any experience we may have of authentic faith in such witnesses as it is our fortune to meet. We have all known beings in whom faith has withstood trials to which it would have seemed natural for it to succumb; we could have gone further and said that their faith emerged even strengthened from these trials. These are the real witnesses. But it is also true that there is always a possibility of shirking or rejecting testimonies such as these, which make us ashamed of our own lack of faith. Then we shall be induced to put in the notion of some sort of vital lies, in Ibsen's sense, which we say these unfortunate people have had to credit in order to live. To acknowledge these testimonies in the fullness of their significance is in some way to become witnesses ourselves. We might add that if we do acknowledge them, it is because we are ourselves upheld, however feebly, by the exigence to which these witnesses have, for their part, given a full response.

It goes without saying that our opponent will not agree that he has lost the case: he will retort that the fault in our reasoning lies in arguing from the testimony (fictitiously considered as an effect) to the existence of the being about whom such testimony is given. But the same answer will always hold good: the objection implies a fictitious idea of some exteriority of the witness in relation to that about which he testifies. The Christian idea of an indwelling of Christ in the man who is completely faithful to Him, an idea which corresponds exactly in the religious order to the position which I am trying to define on the philosophical plane, involves a categorical rejection of this purely imaginary way of picturing it. Just as I spoke in my first series of lectures of creative fidelity, so now we are concerned with creative testifying. But we must repeat once more that creation is never a production; it implies an active receptivity, and in this connection any idealist interpretation must be resolutely rejected.

We are progressing, accordingly, towards the idea that a theology which is not based on testimony must be looked at with suspicion; to be more precise, it can hardly have more than a negative import, to which, however, we should be wrong in attaching too little weight. We may perhaps find something to illustrate this if we go back to the idea of trial or ordeal as we have been using it in this chapter.

Again it is the causalist interpretation that we have to rule out. By that I mean that it would be hopeless to imagine some sort of celestial schoolmaster who sets real spiritual tests which his creatures have to take; and it may be profitable to give more explicit reasons why such a conception would be offensive to religious consciousness. The chief argument seems to me to be this: the examiner who sets a test treats his subject not as a being, but as a case – in other words, here we are confronted with purely abstract relations between an expert and the answers to an expert's inquiries. Fatherhood, however, is something quite different, and excludes such relations. It is true that it is always possible for the father to behave as a schoolmaster or pedantic examiner, but that possibility depends on his having a pretentious self-sufficiency which fatherhood should exclude. Now, it is precisely as *fatherhood in its purity* that the relation between the living God and the faithful should be conceived. One might also say that human fatherhood is conceived on the model of divine fatherhood, and not conversely; but here we are concerned with fatherhood taken in its full richness. If we want to clarify these ideas, we have only to compare the father in the parable of the prodigal son with the Roman *paterfamilias*. In the parable fatherhood appears in what I may call its supra-juridical fullness, and that is precisely why we can see it as being divine instead of consisting in simple relations of power and right, or in a mere bodily belonging as considered from the sociological point of view. We may add that even if we were to find in pre-Christian or extra-Christian history some example of paternal love as it shines through the parable, we should have to see in it only glimmerings through space and time of the pure light which lies at the heart of the gospel.

But if we refuse to think of trial as a contrivance of which God makes use, what becomes of its metaphysical status? We must, I think, say that we can think of circumstance – accident, for example – only as a link in some chain of events. But this is relative to a particular way of conceiving the world, the way of thinking which is chosen or adopted by a consciousness careful to depersonalize itself as much as possible. From the ultimate metaphysical point of view the mistake lies, no doubt, in raising this type of thought to an absolute position. We must keep in mind the possibility of other interpretations. I have often found it useful to take an illustration from music, and I shall do so again; I can to some extent analyze an orchestral score without the meaning of the music being completely grasped by me – the word *meaning* is of course inaccurate, let us rather say the gist of it; by which I mean that the music may *say nothing to me*. It is still foreign to me; I stop short at describing it, though my description may be as minute as you please. But for depersonalized thought accident enters into the matter, in conditions which are capable of being reconstructed objectively, e.g., the motor-cyclist was riding too fast, he did not pay attention to the lights, and so on. Similarly, a discord can be interpreted in a merely contrapuntal way by a technician who does not recognize its musical value; whereas a musician does not see it as in any way contingent, but rather as the expression of an inner necessity to which, however, no strictly logical character can be attached. At the same time, this comparison itself falls far short of adequacy. We are so situated in the world that it is impossible for us to raise ourselves on this earth to a mode of understanding events which allows their intimate meaning to be intuitively apparent to us. The most one could say – and that only tentatively – is that as we approach the apparent term of our existence we are progressively more capable of seeing ourselves in a light which allows the hidden meaning of events to filter through. [MBII, pp. 131–142]

* * *

4. Prayer

Prayer, as we see it practiced by the most fervent souls, can in no instance be understood as containing in itself its own granting. On the contrary, it may be thought of as depending on the mysterious will of an incomprehensible power whose plans we cannot fathom. The man who is praying thinks of himself as quite uncertain, however hopeful he may be, of the answer which will be made to his prayer.

Should we, then, say that in as much as the praying consciousness takes heed of its uncertainty, it is laboring under an error or delusion, that to some extent it is misled by an anthropomorphic realism; and add that it is the philosopher's business to expose and denounce this delusion? That would be an extremely dangerous position to take up, I must admit. It amounts to giving primacy to philosophy in matters that concern religious life, and the final result of that is to depreciate the latter. That is what the intellectualist teachings of the past, particularly those derived from Spinoza, have done. The philosophy of existence, as I have tried to define it, cannot but be completely dissatisfied with such a devaluation.

The truth is probably that when prayer is pure – and I need not elaborate again the meaning of purity in this context – it cannot be thought of as remaining unanswered; it cannot be like a letter which the addressee has left unopened or thrown by mistake or without bothering into the waste paper basket. The believer cannot feel sure that he has a living relation with God, without, by reason of that certainty, having grounds for a pronouncement on the manner in which empirically his prayer will be granted. It would seem that what is definitely excluded is the possibility that his prayer may be treated as though it had never been made. This is only to be expected insofar as we do not ourselves take prayer seriously or as our manner of praying is a justification, by way of a salving of our conscience, of this sort of more or less unacknowledged contempt of prayer.

From this again we can see, and this time indirectly, how we are in a position to distinguish what authentic prayer can be. It can be neither the request which we discussed before, nor a mechanical recitation of formulae. We could add that it is nothing if not a certain very humble and fervent way of *uniting oneself with* . . . though we must admit that that phrase itself is still inadequate. The fact is that in a general way it is almost impossible for us to think of union except in relation to what is akin to us, in which case we integrate ourselves into a whole whose elements are homogeneous. In the case of prayer such a union cannot be thought of. Here the mystery lies in that I have to merge in something which infinitely transcends me, and at first it seems impossible to conceive such a thing. It might perhaps be suggested that the union we claim might be interpreted as a surrender – but a surrender to what? To a will whose ends and whose very nature go infinitely beyond anything we can conceive. But would not that amount to a blind unconditional surrender? "Whatever you may will, your will shall be mine."

It is not to be denied that the believer feels that this absolute submission seems to be required of him by the being in whom he has faith, but it would appear extremely difficult to maintain this formula, and for a very simple reason: in the world in which we have, literally, been put, it is extremely difficult for us to distinguish what is willed and what is only permitted. It is quite impossible to imagine that any circumstance at all should be looked on as willed for its own sake, simply because I am faced by that circumstance; otherwise we might end in approving the manifestly absurd attitude of those who think it sacrilegious to treat a disease medically or to cure it by an operation. (Such an attitude, moreover, is unanimously condemned as unreasonable nowadays, except for one or two sects, and one might well go further into the reasons for that condemnation.)

Reflection seems to make it quite clear that we have to force our way between two errors which are of very different natures, and the path is narrow and full of obstacles. One of the errors lies in taking up a position exclusively within the sphere of causality, which is to say of technique. From that point of view, prayer would appear as a pure epiphenomenon, or rather as auto-suggestion. The other error, which I pointed out just above, lies on the contrary in neglecting, that is to say, in dismissing as non-existent, the correlations which reason enables us to disclose. The truth would seem to be that we must try to understand how "the spirit of prayer" can be fitted in with the series of positive steps which reason demands in any given situation. To take a very simple example: we may readily imagine that a surgeon who is a believer may feel the need for prayer before he undertakes a particularly difficult operation. It is by no means impossible to imagine how this prayer may open and clear the road for his action. But the situation with which he has to deal cannot really be thought of *either* as having been willed or produced by the divine will, considered as a pure agent, *or* as being a mere link in a chain of cause and effect – which is what a metaphysic determinist in inspiration would maintain that it is. By this second hypothesis the only way out would be in the direction of a stoicism which would disregard the situation as being quite indifferent in its bearing upon a certain inalienable essence in the subject. Ultimately, however, this is sheer fiction, though it may be a very noble fiction. To take an extreme example, a man suffering from an incurable disease cannot take refuge in this lofty *apatheia*; or, if we can imagine that he might, he will always be liable to entertain doubts of the validity of such an attitude. The truth is rather that he should look at the position as touching him very fundamentally. Can we, then, see how what I have called the spirit of prayer may be manifested in a similar case? Or again, that union of which we said that it could not be reduced to the union which can be achieved between finite beings?

The spirit of prayer, I think, may first be defined negatively as the rejection of a temptation; and the temptation would consist in being shut in on oneself in pride or despair, two things which are closely connected. Positively, however, is not the spirit of prayer seen to be primarily a receptive disposition towards everything which can detach me from myself and from my tendency to blind myself to my own failings? It is not, however, simply a spirit of detachment; the man who is concerned only with abstracting from himself is still but at the beginning of a road which climbs infinitely higher. We may note, moreover, that the progress which is possible is not required by anything resembling a dialectical necessity. It is an unfortunate delusion, fostered by philosophers like Hegel, that belief entails such a necessity. This delusion is tied up, also, with a phenomenon of pure substitution. Simple representations arranged by thought to suit itself, as one might deal out a pack of cards, are substituted for the real phases of a development which is that of the existent. All one can say is that when thought works a *posteriori* on a development which is in reality a conversion . . . it is always on the road to interpreting it dialectically. . . .

. . . When we speak of the spirit of prayer, can we mean anything but an interior disposition? Do we not feel that we are enclosed in a circle in which consciousness seems to come back on itself? Once more secondary reflection has to be called in. To what do we oppose this "anything but"? Surely it is the idea we rejected earlier of a sort of external relation between the person who prays and the person who should hear his prayer but may be absent? But we must repeat and emphasize what we said above: if prayer is to be recognized as real, it must be possible to mark out a road to serve as an intermediary. Every time, however, that we try to advance along this road we are open to the temptation of putting forward again the dilemma which we have been concerned to circumvent. We must realize from the start that the more we look at the believer from a monadist point of view, the more insoluble and even, no doubt, meaningless, the problem will appear. . . . Prayer is possible only when intersubjectivity is recognized, where it is operative. We must, it is true, keep well in mind that intersubjectivity can never be looked upon as a mode of structure which can be stated or verified in any way; that would be to make it into a spurious sort of objectivity. The positive corollary of this is that the intersubjective can only be acknowledged freely, and that implies further that it is always within our power to deny it. I can always behave as though I had in reality no means of access to the reality of another, as though the other were only a bunch of possibilities to be made use of, or of threats to be neutralized. There we have a practical solipsism, and this solipsism can not only be overt but even, if I may so put it, can provide its own justification. It is only, however, the man who has contrived to make his way into the intersubjective sphere who can see this practical solipsism as nothing but a blinding, and a blinding which is at least to some extent voluntary. One may, in fact, say almost with certainty that there is nobody who has all his life been so unlucky as to have found it impossible ever to unite himself with another, or obliged to deny the other as a real presence. [MBII, pp. 102–107]

*   *   *

5. Creation

My deepest and most unshakable conviction – and if it is heretical, so much the worse for orthodoxy – is, that whatever all the thinkers and doctors have said, it is not God's will at all to be loved by us *against* the Creation, but rather glorified *through* the Creation and with the Creation as our starting-point. That is why I find so many devotional books intolerable. The God who is set up against the Creation and who is somehow jealous of his own works is, to my mind, nothing but an idol. [BH, p. 135]

*   *   *

6. Catholics and Protestants

Few controversies to my mind are more futile and ultimately more exasperating than those which periodically oppose Catholics to Protestants, both of whom are nevertheless endowed with the same good will, with the same desire for mutual understanding, but who try to sharpen the nature of their agreement and disagreement. As soon as the Catholic declares to the Protestant that he, as a Catholic, or more precisely, the Church, is a guardian of a universal truth of which the Protestant grasps only a few fragments which are tainted with error – in short, when he wholly denies that he is on the same level as his adversary – he destroys the conditions which are requisite for debate, and even though the encounter takes place under seemingly favorable auspices, it is practically impossible for it not to end in bitterness, despair, and incurable misunderstanding. No doubt the latter is not altogether avoidable in fact if not in principle; yet the fact that Christians do find it impossible to understand one another is such a scandal from the viewpoint of the gospel that it must be rejected with the same unequivocal and abiding refusal that evil in its various forms would wrest from us. [CF, pp. 191–192]

Chapter 5

Critique of Contemporary Culture

Marcel expresses in his work his worries about the growth of technology, and the increased emphasis on materialism in modern life. This theme is the subject of these two selections from his book, Man against Mass Society, *which is a sustained discussion of this topic.*

In the first selection, he questions materialist consumerism, which tends to reduce human beings to the status of things, an approach that threatens our freedom. It is necessary, he argues, to turn to the transcendent, which is also in itself a protest that we don't fully belong to the world of objects; an appeal to the transcendent dimension of human existence, broadly understood, is the only way we can remain free. Marcel links these ideas with the notions of creativity and intersubjectivity, and notes that the temptation to succumb to modern materialism is strong.

In the second selection, he continues the theme that our great technical progress often leads to our spiritual degradation. But this does not mean that we should reject technology, or that we can turn back the clock. He holds that technical progress is not necessarily negative in itself, and is not of necessity detrimental to the life of the spirit; nevertheless, it often is, because it tempts us to substitute material satisfaction for spiritual joy, which can lead to a general pessimistic attitude toward life in general, and an inability to cope without material comforts or distractions.

He concludes this selection with a number of penetrating reflections on the effect of materialism on various aspects of modern life.

*   *   *

1. On Materialism, Degradation, and Transcendence

What we have to recognize is this. Thanks to the techniques of degradation it is creating and perfecting, a materialistic mode of thought, in our time, is showing itself capable of bringing into being a world which more and more *tends to verify its own materialistic postulates.* I mean that a human being who has undergone a certain type of psychological manipulation tends progressively to be reduced to the status of a mere *thing*; a psychic thing, of course, but nevertheless a thing which falls quite tidily within the province of the theories elaborated by an essentially materialistic psychology. This assertion of mine is, of course, obviously ambiguous; it does not mean that this materialistic psychology, with however startling powers of reductive transformation it may become endowed, will ever be of a nature to grasp and reveal to us reality as it is in itself. Rather, my assertion emphasizes the fact that there is nothing surprising for a philosophy like my own, a philosophy of man as a being in a situation, in the fact that man depends, to a very great degree, on the idea he has of himself and that this idea cannot be degraded without at the same time degrading man. This is one more reason, and on the face of things the most serious and imperative reason, for condemning materialistic thinking, root and branch. And it is relevant to note here that in our day the materialistic attitude has acquired a virulence and a cohesion which it was far from possessing in the last century. It was a common spectacle then to see thinkers who regarded themselves as thoroughly imbued with materialistic principles showing in their personal lives all the scrupulosity of Kantian rigorists.

It may seem that I am rather straying here from the question which I set out to answer at the beginning of this chapter, "What is a free man?" But this is not in fact by any means the case, for it is very important for us to recognize, whatever fancies certain thinkers incapable of the least coherence may have had about this question, that a materialistic conception of the universe is radically incompatible with the idea of a free man: more precisely, that, in a society ruled by materialistic principles, freedom is transmuted into its opposite, or becomes merely the most treacherous and deceptive of empty slogans.

Theoretically, of course, we can imagine the possibility of man's preserving a minimum of independence even in a society ruled on materialistic principles; but, as we ought to be immediately aware, this possibility is an evanescent one, implying contradictions: for freedom in such a society would consist, if I may put it so, in rendering oneself sufficiently insignificant to escape the attention of the men in power. But is it not fairly obvious that this wish for insignificance, supposing even that it is a wish that can be put into effect, is already in a sense a suicidal wish? In such a society, the mere keeping, for instance, of an intimate diary might be a capital crime, and one does not see why, by the use of tape recorders and tapped telephones, as well as by various quite conceivable extensions of the use of radio, it should not be quite possible to keep the police well informed about the thoughts and the feelings of any individual whatsoever. From the point of view of the individual in such a society, there is no conceivable way out at all: private life, as such, does not exist any more.

But let us imagine, then, the situation of our own country immediately after a *putsch* or a *coup d'état:* if rebellion is futile, and a retreat into insignificance impracticable, what, supposing that we are fully aware of our situation, does there remain for us to do? At the risk of discontenting and even of shocking those who still tend to think of solutions for political problems in terms of positive action, I shall say that in that region all the ways of escape seem to me to be barred. Our only recourse can be to the Transcendent: but what does that mean? "The transcendent," "transcendence," these are words which among philosophers and intellectuals, for a good many years past, have been strangely misused. When I myself speak here of a recourse to the transcendent, I mean, as concretely as possible, that our only chance in the sort of horrible situation I have imagined is to appeal, I should perhaps *not* say to a power, but rather to a level of being, an order of the spirit, which is also the level and order of grace, of mercy, of charity; and to proclaim, while there is still time, that is to say before the state's psychological manipulations have produced in us the alienation from our true selves that we fear, that we repudiate *in advance* the deeds and the acts that may be obtained from us by any sort of constraint whatsoever. We solemnly affirm, by this appeal to the transcendent, that the reality of our selves lies *beyond* any such acts and any such words. It will be said, no doubt, that by this gesture we are giving ourselves a very ideal, a very unreal, sort of satisfaction; but to say so is to fail to recognize the real nature of the thought which I am groping to put into shape. What we have to do is to proclaim that we do *not* belong entirely to the world of objects to which men are seeking to assimilate us, in which they are straining to imprison us. To put it very concretely indeed, we have to proclaim that this life of ours, which it has now become technically possible to make into a hideous and grimacing parody of all our dreams, may in reality be only the most insignificant aspect of a grand process unfolding itself far beyond the boundaries of the visible world. In other words, this amounts to saying that *all philosophies of immanence have had their day*, that in our own day they have revealed their basic unreality or, what is infinitely more serious, their complicity with those modern idolatries which it is our duty to denounce without pity: the idolatry of race, the idolatry of class. I should add here that even the authentic religions may become similarly degraded in their very principle of being. They too can degenerate into idolatries; especially where the will to power is waiting to corrupt them; and this, alas, is almost invariably the case when the Church becomes endowed with temporal authority.

But we are now on the road towards a number of pretty positive conclusions. I should formulate them as follows: a man cannot be free or remain free, except in the degree to which he remains linked with that which transcends him, whatever the particular form of that link may be: for it is pretty obvious that the form of the link need not reduce itself to official and canonical prayers. I should say that in the case particularly of the true artist in paint, or stone, or music, or words, this relationship to the transcendent is something that is experienced in the most authentic and profound way. I am supposing, of course, that he does not yield to the innumerable temptations to which the artist is exposed today: the temptation to startle, to innovate at all costs, to shut oneself up in a private world leaving as few channels as possible open for communication with the world of eternal forms, and so on. But nothing could be more false and more dangerous than to base on these observations of mine some sort of neo-aestheticism. We have to recognize that there are modes of creation which do not belong to the aesthetic order, and which are within the reach of everybody; and it is in so far as he is a creator, at however humble a level, that any man at all can recognize his own freedom. It would be necessary, moreover, to show that the idea of being creative, taken in this quite general sense, always implies the idea of being open towards others: that openness I have called in my Gifford Lectures, intersubjectivity, whether that is conceived as *agape* (charity) or *philia* (attachment): these two notions, in any case, I think, tend ultimately to converge. But what must be stated as forcibly as possible is that societies built on a materialistic basis, whatever place they tactfully leave for a collective and at bottom purely animal exaltation, sin radically against intersubjectivity; they exclude it in principle; and it is because they exclude it, that they grub up every possible freedom by its roots.

It is quite conceivable – and I put this idea forward not as an abstract hypothesis but as a familiar fact – that in a country enslaved by a totalitarian power, a man might find himself constrained, not merely in order to live but in order to withdraw his dependants from a state of absolute wretchedness, to accept, for instance, a job with the security police: a job which might compel him to carry out acts absolutely repugnant to his conscience. Is mere refusal to carry out such acts a solution to his problem? We may doubt this, for the very reason that such a refusal might entail dire consequences not only for the man himself but for his innocent dependants. But it could happen that the man who accepted such a job might make a religious vow to use the share of power which he has been given so much as possible to help the very people of whom he was officially the persecutor. Such a vow, with the creative power that it re-bestows on him who makes it, is a concrete example of that recourse to the transcendent of which I spoke earlier on.

But it is obvious that there is nothing in such an extremely particular case out of which any general rule can be framed. A rigoristic moral formalism, an attempt to bring all human acts under very general rules, ceases almost entirely to be acceptable as soon as one becomes aware of that element of the unique and the incommensurable which is the portion of every concrete being, confronted with a concrete situation. No two beings, and no two situations, are really commensurable with each other. To become aware of this fact is to undergo a sort of crisis. But it is with this crisis in our moral awareness as a starting point, that there becomes possible that cry from us towards the creative principle, and that demand by it on us, which each must answer in his own way, if he does not wish to become an accomplice of what Simone Weil called "the gross beast." In our world as it is today there can be hardly any set of circumstances in which we may not be forced to ask ourselves whether, through our free choice, through our particular decisions, we are not going to make ourselves guilty of just such a complicity. [*MMS*, pp. 17–25]

* * *

2. Technology and the Materialistic life

In the second place, I fear that we must go further than this and ask ourselves whether there is not something in this mechanical method of diffusing thought which almost inevitably degrades whatever message men are seeking to diffuse. Moreover, I would say that it is not very difficult to find out the causes of this inevitable degradation, by the radio, of thought. Do they not lie in the fact that in the realm of radio man is attempting, without, however, this involving any real effort on his part, to transcend his human condition and the limitations it entails? It is, of course, not difficult to conceive that a saint might by some sudden miracle be invested, at least for a moment passing like a lightning flash, with the gift of ubiquity: that would only be a spatial transposition of his gift of charity, which in itself is independent of the *here* and the *now*. But how can we admit that such a miraculous gift can, without losing all its potency, be vested in the ordinary man? How can we allow that it is quite safe for any individual, whoever he is, to be granted the gift of being everywhere at once in return for the payment of an annual rent for radio time? Is there not a sort of usurpation here? And on the other hand do we not feel that something which is advantageous or good in itself, once it has been usurped, is liable in the long run to be put to evil uses?

I am not at all sure that all this could not be formulated in a much more general fashion: I am not sure that every kind of technical progress may not entail, for the individual who takes advantage of it *without having had any share in the effort at overcoming difficulties of which such a progress is the culmination*, the payment of a heavy price, of which a certain degradation at the spiritual level is the natural expression. Obviously, this does not mean that history can start moving backwards and that we ought to break all the machines: it means merely that, as Bergson with so much profundity observed, every kind of outward technical progress ought to be balanced in man by an effort at inner conquest, directed towards an ever greater self-mastery. Unhappily, what we still have to ask is whether for an individual who every day takes more and more advantage of the facilities which technical progress has put at his disposal, such an effort at self-mastery does not become more and more difficult. There is certainly every reason to suppose that it does. In our contemporary world it may be said that the more a man becomes dependent on the gadgets whose smooth functioning assures him a tolerable life at the material level, the more estranged he becomes from an awareness of his inner reality. I should be tempted to say that the center of gravity of such a man and his balancing point tend to become external to himself: that he projects himself more and more into objects, into the various pieces of apparatus on which he depends for his existence. It would be no exaggeration to say that the more progress "humanity" as an abstraction makes towards the mastery of nature, the more actual individual men tend to become slaves of this very conquest.

At the point we have now reached in this argument, broad horizons open out before us. We see superimposed on the relatively simple and particular notion of techniques aimed at degrading special groups of human beings, a notion of a much more general sort: we are about to ask ourselves whether, in certain conditions of which we must of course get a more exact idea, a technical progress which seems to be, of its nature, indifferent to moral values, but which is on the other hand the expression at the material level of a genuine intellectual conquest, is not itself in danger of becoming a method of human degradation; and indeed, when I have concluded this investigation of mine, it will be relevant to ask whether the fact that technical progress seems to be culminating today in the invention of more and more formidable instruments of destruction can be imputed to a mere chance concurrence of circumstances.

We ought to insist, however, that there would be no point in regarding either technical progress in general, or the progress of some particular technique, as having of its very nature a necessarily negative value for the spirit. It would be more precise to say that technical progress in the strict sense is a good thing, both good in itself, and good because it is the incarnation of a genuine power that lies in human reason: good even because it introduces into the apparent disorder of the outer world a principle of intelligibility. But the question we are faced with is this: what are the effects (not the necessary effects, but the probable effects) of technical progress on the man who takes advantage of it without having helped in any way to achieve it? Ought not the observations which I have already roughly outlined to direct us towards a deeper truth? Does not the invasion of our life by techniques today tend to substitute satisfaction at a material level for spiritual joy, dissatisfaction at a material level for spiritual disquiet? And do not the satisfied and the unsatisfied tend to come together in a common mediocrity? The fact is that to the average man today, whose inner life tends too often to be a rather dim affair in any case, technical progress seems the infallible method by which he can achieve a sort of generalized comfort, apart from which he finds it impossible to imagine happiness. I am bearing in mind also that this generalized comfort, with its appurtenances – standardized amusements, and so on – seems the only possible way to make life tolerable, when life is no longer considered as a divine gift, but rather as a "dirty joke." The existence of a widely diffused pessimism, at the level of the sneer and the oath rather than that of sighs and weeping, seems to me a fundamental given fact about contemporary humanity; and it seems to me that it is in the perspective of this widely diffused pessimism, a pessimism not so much thought out as retched forth, a sort of physical nausea at life, that we ought to consider such a serious and significant contemporary fact as the prevalence, for instance, of abortion.

Let us recall also the relevant fact that in an absurd or chaotic world technical achievements tend to seem more and more the chief, if not the only, mark of man's superiority to the animals. In this exaltation of techniques there might, of course, be a Promethean defiance, not without its own greatness and nobility. But, at the level of the consumer, such a defiance is degraded and perverted. Quite aside from the fact that technical progress, considered from the consumer's point of view, encourages a kind of laziness, it also fosters resentment and envy. These passions center themselves on definite material objects, whose possession usually does not seem to be linked to any definite personal superiority, not even that superiority of refined taste which a lover of prints or china may show in building up his collection. Where a frigidaire or a radio-gramophone are in question, the very ideas of "having" and "possessing" acquire a sense which is at once provocative of bad feeling and spiritually hollow: "He has the good luck to possess that gadget, and he didn't do anything for it; it does belong to him, of course, but it might just as well belong to me, and that would be fairer." Between my sort of mechanical apparatus and its possessor there cannot be established that living, that almost latently spiritual relationship, that exists, for instance, between a small-holder and his piece of land: that exists there, because the very notion of the cultivation of the ground implies, also, the notion of an extraordinary exchange – a mutual, patient traffic between the land's fruitfulness and the peasant's care. But is it not rather the case that in the world where technique is triumphant this idea of "exchange," though still persistent, has lost its old values: just because exchange in the true sense is not something mechanical? It implies, rather, an endless pos-sibility of disappointment; for the owner of a vineyard, for instance, who has tended his vines with loving care throughout the year, may at the last moment see his grapes destroyed by a hailstorm. For him and for his like, there can be no guarantee of security. In the realm of mechanical technique, in theory at least, there is no danger of anything so distressing and shocking happening: in theory, I say, for in practice the effects of a bad harvest or an epidemic can impinge even on this protected area. But obviously the ideal at which technical progress is aiming is that of bringing into being a privileged realm: one on which these impingements of the unpredictable will no longer have any effect, and where guarantees of security will be utterly reliable.

Now, that the sort of thing I described a moment ago can happen to the peasant is undoubtedly distressing and shocking; but, on the other hand, experience seems to show us that as soon as a preoccupation with security begins to dominate human life, the scope of human life itself tends to be diminished. Life, as it were, tends to shrink back on itself, to wither. One reason for this may be that the powers of initiative, among those who are not equipped to contribute effectively to scientific and technical progress, tend to exercise themselves as it were on the edge of things and even to degenerate into a mere power of subversion. That might be one of the more fundamental reasons why a period in history of highly developed techniques tends also to become a period of revolution. But we ought to ask ourselves also whether the will to subversion, in our world today, may not be linked to a precisely opposite disposition: to a sort of petty conservatism, narrowed down to the notion of conserving the individual's own skin; for the spirit that used to inspire a more generous type of popular conservatism, the spirit that inspired the workman to bring up a large family, is dying away, just where it used properly to exercise itself. It no longer makes men want to bring up and educate many children; it transfers itself to a level of mere talk where it is lost in words and smoke or, worse still, it expresses itself in physical violence and finally in the persecution of one human group by another one.

In such a train of events (the degradation of the conservative spirit in workmen from care for a family to political rant and finally to brutish violence), the degrading side of technical progress is displayed with the utmost clarity. The notion of life is degraded in the first place, and all the other degradations quite naturally follow. We might even ask whether the man who lives as a servant of technical progress does not come to regard life as a technique mainly: a very imperfect one, where slapdash work and botching are still the rule. Given such a point of view, how could such a man fail to claim for himself the right to interfere with the onflow of life, just as one dams a river? Before he decides to start a baby "on the way," he will make careful calculations, just as if he were buying a motorcycle; he will try to estimate the annual expense as exactly as possible; foreseeing illnesses and doctors' bills in one case; wear and tear and garage expenses in the other. Fairly frequently, instead of a baby, he will decide, by way of economy, on a little dog. It costs less; and if the bills at the veterinary surgeon's grow too big, it can always be put painlessly out of the way. So far, to be sure, we have not envisaged this possibility in the case of sickly small children.

We could push this analysis much farther, and in quite other directions; at the level not of the individual and the family but of the State and international life, what are the points of impact of a process which tends more and more towards the identification of science and power, at a level where the difference between science and technique in some regions of science at least, is becoming negligible? In a world in which the absolute hegemony of States or groups of States is being affirmed, how almost irresistible must be the temptation to confiscate new inventions, new patents, for the benefit of these monstrous powers! But competition between States for inventions must tend more and more to augment, the more intense it becomes, that collective application of technical power with which today the very notion of science tends to be confused. Just as, in the case of its effects on the individual, technical progress would be wholly a good thing if it were to remain at the services of a spiritual activity directed towards higher ends, so, at the international level, technical progress could be considered as a priceless gift if it were to be exercised on behalf of a unified mankind, or rather on behalf of mankind working together. But when this is not the case either for the individual or in relation to the great human collectivities, it becomes immediately obvious that technical progress is bound to be transformed from a blessing into a curse.

For that matter, there is not in this process, as some simple-minded people think, some sort of unintelligible calamity, like a cyclone or a cholera epidemic (which of course are neither of them strictly unintelligible either), but rather a price we have to pay for what, in a vocabulary unfamiliar to technical experts, we must simply call *sin*. One of the misfortunes of our time is that the use of this word is almost the private preserve of the clergy, whom hardly anybody listens to, and who, indeed, do not always know how to transcend the limits of a mode of speech, ancient and respectable, no doubt, but which seems sometimes quite unable to get to grips with real and visible evils. Once more, I ought to emphasize here that there would be no point in thinking of technical progress as being in itself the expression of sin. It is clear enough, indeed, that, at our present period in history, as soon as the techniques on which civilized life rests yield before hostile pressures, a return to barbarous conditions sets in with disconcerting rapidity. On the other hand, it is also clear that technical progress is increasingly tempting man to claim for his achievements at this level an intrinsic value that cannot really belong to them. Quite simply, we can say that there is a danger of technical progress making men into idolaters.

If men are generally unaware of this danger, it is because they are deceived by their own childish notion of idolatry. Idolatry is something that savages do! It consists of adoring queer little fetishes! How could the mechanic or the emancipated "little man," who pride themselves in believing nothing, be idolaters? Have they not freed themselves from all superstitions? But their delusion consists precisely in failing to recognize that superstition can work itself into the very substance of the mind: to use an unpleasant image, one might say that superstition becomes encysted in the modern consciousness, instead of breaking out in a warning rash on the surface. The man who "believes in nothing" does not really exist, any more than the man who clings to nothing, who holds to nothing: and to believe in something and to cling or hold to it are at bottom very much the same mental act. People forget this, because they tend to lump "believing in" something together with "forming" or "holding" an "opinion" about it. That, however, is a blunder: for it does very often happen that our "opinions," under analysis, can be seen to be not mental acts but mere mental habits. In practice, they reduce themselves to things which we habitually say in a certain context, without asking ourselves what our words mean or how they would be applied in the actual world: in fact, we should often feel "caught out" if someone asked us to put our opinions into practice. On the other hand, we really only "believe in" something which we do in practice cling to or hold to: now, to cling or hold to something is to have some sort of living link with it; the man who believes in nothing, like the man who clings to nothing, can have no such links. But such a man is notional or even chimerical. He cannot actually exist. Existence without living links is not concretely conceivable. It is not among real possibilities.

. . . To sum up our drift so far and to prepare the way for the general conclusions that are going to be forced on us, let us make the following statement: a civilization in which technical progress is tending to emancipate itself more and more from speculative knowledge, and finally to question the traditional rights of speculative knowledge, a civilization which, one may say, finally denies the place of contemplation and shuts out the very possibility of contemplation, such a civilization, I say, sets us inevitably on the road towards a philosophy which is not so much a *love of wisdom* as a *hatred of wisdom*: we ought rather to call it a misosophy. For, in the last analysis, we may ask ourselves how it is possible on such foundations to erect anything at all resembling what has traditionally been understood by the word "wisdom." It seems to me, for instance, almost certain that the notion of authentic wisdom implies references to a level of reality which is wholly left out of the calculations of a man like Sartre when he makes his contrast between "being-in-itself" (corresponding to what has been traditionally called "matter") and "being-for-itself," corresponding not so much to what has traditionally been called "mind" as to a kind of interior collapse. Let us remember in addition, that Sartre at all times and in all situations is very ready to attack what he calls "serious-mindedness." But this serious-mindedness is something which the very notion of wisdom, if wisdom is not to be degraded into a sort of sneering buffoonery, does most definitely imply. This is true even of pessimistic thinkers of the great tradition; for them, there is at least *something* which must be taken seriously, and that is the verdict which the wise man or the holy man finds himself forced to pass on a world of illusion and madness; but surely this verdict itself requires the wise man or the saint to transcend the world of illusion and madness – and transcendence, in this sense, is something for the possibility of which Sartre and his friends seem to me to make no allowances.

In this chapter, then, we have started by considering techniques of degradation at their most deliberate and systematic, the techniques which aim at degrading some given category of men – of degrading them *in their own eyes*. It is easy to see that it is only possible to make use of such techniques in a world in which universal values are being systematically trampled underfoot; and by "universal values" here, I do not wish to emphasize particularly notions like "goodness as such," "truth as such" – that is a type of Platonism of which I am hardly an adherent. It is not a matter merely of the *idea* of the good or the true being trampled on, but of these values being trampled on in their living scope and actual relations: being trampled on in so far as they confer on human existence its proper dignity – in so far as they confer that on *every* human existence. In this connection, I should notice in passing, it is quite impossible to acquit Nietzsche of a certain at least indirect responsibility for the horrors of which we have been, and still are, the witnesses. We ought not, of course, to be deceived by a philosopher's special vocabulary; and when Nietzsche talked about getting "beyond good and evil," we should recognize that he wanted to lay the foundations for a higher kind of good. It is none the less true – and either Nietzsche failed to perceive this, or he was very wrong in thinking himself not bound to take it into consideration – that, at the level of experience, Nietzsche's "beyond" becomes a "beneath"; his way up is, in practice, a way down: not a transcendence of ordinary moral categories but, to use a word coined by Jean Wahl, a transdescendence from them. [*MMS*, pp. 55–67]

Chapter 6

On the Role of Drama

Here we have the good fortune to listen in on a conversation between Marcel and Paul Ricoeur. Ricoeur recorded six conversations with Marcel about various aspects of his work. This conversation focuses on Marcel's drama. Ricoeur asks him about the connection between his dramatic work and his philosophical work, and his focus on the concrete real life situations the characters in his plays find themselves in, as they deal with typical existential situations, like anguish, despair and death. Marcel refers along the way to several examples of themes in his plays which he later developed in his philosophical work.

* * *

Conversation between Paul Ricoeur and Gabriel Marcel

PAUL RICOEUR: Our last discussion brought us to an important threshold in your work, drama. Everything in your work comes from drama and everything leads to it as well, especially the analysis of those experiences you have called "ontological," insofar as these experiences have a dramatic character.

In *Being and Having* you write: "the fact that despair is possible is a central datum here. Man is capable of despair, capable of embracing death, of embracing his own death." And elsewhere: "Metaphysics ought to take up its position just there, face to face with despair: metaphysics as an exorcism of despair." How do you consider your plays now? How do you see the relation between your dramatic work and your philosophical work?

GABRIEL MARCEL: I am very glad you are asking me this question because I believe it is the most important one, and it is one of those points where there have probably been the most serious misunderstandings, particularly among theater people who have not taken the trouble to really read my work. The truth is that the connection between philosophy and drama in my case is the closest, the most intimate possible.

Briefly, I would say that my philosophy is existential to the degree that it is simultaneously drama, that is, dramatic creation. What has struck me very much these last years while reflecting on my work is the fact that existence, or, if you will, the existing subject, can be adequately thought only where the thinking subject is allowed to speak. If we speak of this existing subject in some other way, we insist *in the words* on its subjective character, but by the very fact that we are speaking of it we inevitably objectify it and consequently distort it.

Of course this is an a posteriori viewpoint. Chronologically, I did not proceed this way at all. And besides – I will have a chance later on perhaps to repeat this – I was thinking about drama a great deal before I knew or suspected what philosophy is. But if you ask me how I understand this relation today, I would refer to a text that appeared last spring where I developed a comparison which strikes me as quite accurate. Taken as a whole my work can be compared, I think, to a country like Greece, which comprises at the same time a continental part and islands. The continental part is my philosophical writing. Here I find myself to some degree in the company of other thinkers of our time like Jaspers, Buber, and Heidegger. The islands are my plays. Why this comparison? Well, just as it is necessary to make a crossing to get to an island, so to get to my dramatic work, dramatic creation, it is necessary to leave the shore behind. The reflecting subject in some way must leave himself behind, forget himself in order to yield completely, in order to be absorbed in the beings he has conceived and whom he must try to bring to life. And it might be added – I don't think this would be superfluous – that the element which unites the continent and the islands in my work is music. Music is truly the deepest level. In a certain way the priority belongs to music.

PAUL RICOEUR: I think that if drama has had the influence on your philosophy you say it has, then this is so because it has allowed you not only to acknowledge subjectivity by letting the subject speak, but also to encounter individual subjects. In your plays the striking thing is the permanent exercise of what you have called somewhere "that higher justice which resembles charity." Destinies remain intertwined, unseparated. You yourself are never in the position of a judge when you are exercising what I would call the dramatic act.

GABRIEL MARCEL: This seems completely correct to me, and I have attempted elsewhere in recalling my childhood and adolescence to discover the roots of this disposition. There would be more we could say about this. The Dreyfus affair, which I will have a chance to speak about again in another context, played a definite role here.

But there were also family circumstances, in this case a divorce, which were important. I became aware that members of my own family had clearly diverging positions. Each seemed a prisoner of his own viewpoint. So I think I experienced at a very early age the need to raise myself up to a certain level where everyone would be included, where each one would have his place, where each one would in some way be justified.

Moreover, when I consider my first plays, I notice that almost all of them imply the condemnation of the judge, the condemnation of the one who condemns. I think – here I am also anticipating something we will have to talk about later on – that it was in this context that I was first drawn to Christian ethics.

PAUL RICOEUR: If your plays are wholesome and purifying, this is so because they are in no way apologetic. I am very much struck by the fact that in plays like *La Grâce, Le Palais de sable*, and later on *Un Homme de Dieu, La Chapelle ardente*, and *L'Iconoclaste*, the tragedy consists in the fact that nothing is solved for the characters. And nothing is resolved because the bearers of meaning or hope are always challengeable, or even suspect, sometimes even unbearable. I spoke of the wholesomeness of your plays. Actually, your plays serve to get rid of phantoms, to exorcise them, preparing the way for what the philosopher is not yet able to say. . . .

GABRIEL MARCEL: Yes, several times I have even asked myself – and I would like to know what you think of the matter – if there might not be a certain unexpected analogy between the role of drama in my thought and indirect communication as Kierkegaard conceived it. What strikes me is the interest Kierkegaard had in the theater. The theater is often mentioned in his *Journals*, and I have asked myself occasionally if, in uniting philosophical and dramatic thinking so intimately, I have not in some way accomplished something that Kierkegaard was straining toward. What do you think?

PAUL RICOEUR: I think you are right. But what is characteristic of your particular viewpoint is this justifying comprehension of all the characters. You assume them all simultaneously, without ever being their judge. Now, do you think that all your plays are equally significant in this respect? I am very much struck by a certain alternation between those plays which seem to close in darkness and others where at a certain moment a kind of spark, a kind of lightning flashes out. It seems to me there is something like a pulse in your plays. Sometimes it is that possibility of despair we were speaking about earlier which invades everything; at other times all is swept up in a kind of witness and vague recognition of a mystery which can never be apprehended or possessed. It seems to me then that your plays, besides representing an unresolved tragedy, also express the existential pulse of your philosophy.

GABRIEL MARCEL: I believe that there actually is an alternation, but that it is no more deliberate than it is regular. As a matter of fact, in the book entitled *Le Secret est dans les isles*, this kind of opposition can be found. The first two plays, *Le Dard* and *L'Emissaire*, close with the discovery of a certain light, an obscure light, while the third ends in despair. *La Fin des temps* is one of the darkest plays I have written.

Probably by looking at the web of events we have lived through, one could find something which could help explain this kind of alternation. But I don't believe that a rigorous explanation of it could be given. Of course I would be somewhat distrustful of these plays if in fact each one closed on a happy note: they would seem to me a little mechanical and, because of that, quite suspect.

Among the plays you mentioned, *La Chapelle ardente*, for example, there are some which are certainly very dark plays. I think the spectator can draw something positive from the plays, but this positive element remains implicit. The spectator has to make an effort, a kind of work of reflection, which can be suggested but cannot be insisted on.

PAUL RICOEUR: I think that the theme of death is the one that crystallizes your own inquiry just as it crystallizes the inquiry of the protagonist, of the spectator, and of the reader. You write somewhere that death is "the test of presence," and also that death is "the springboard of an absolute hope." The movement that bears your plays along is that of an "in spite of . . .": in spite of all the denials and the disavowals, despite everything.

And why? Because in your dramatic work death is taken seriously, not just *my* death but, as you say insistently, *your* death. Death then is truly the crisis which completely shatters all faith in existence, all certitude of presence. Your drama, then, is purifying; but even more than purifying, your drama bears witness.

GABRIEL MARCEL: The role of death in my plays is absolutely primary, and so too in a certain way is the role of sickness. Incidentally, this is one of the things which, rather unusually, Pierre Aime Touchard has reproached me for in his book *Dionysos*. He says I have given much too much importance to sickness and death. I confess that this made me smile because I do not believe that one can give too much importance to sickness and death. It is in facing them, in fact, that we are at the very heart of our destiny and of our mystery.

Now there is another point I would like to insist on with regard to this relation between my dramatic and my philosophical work. This is the fact that the dramatic vision, what I see with the help of my characters, has very often been an anticipation of what could appear to me only later on at the philosophical level. A number of examples could be given. You referred to *Le Palais de sable*, which is one of my first published plays. *Le Palais de sable* was written in 1912-13, and what strikes me is that it is clearly in advance of what I was writing at that time in the philosophical register. One sees here, actually, a kind of criticism, from an existential standpoint, of that idealism of faith that I was still somewhat clinging to, a criticism which appeared again a little later on in the first part of the *Metaphysical Journal*.

Already in *La Palais de sable*, without my being able at that time to formulate it for myself in a precise and philosophically rigorous way, the fundamental idea of intersubjectivity appeared, the fact that we are not alone, that whatever we do we are responsible for what happens to others.

Another play often mentioned in books about my work is *L'Iconoclaste*. In the last scene the idea of mystery as clarifying appears in a dramatic context, mystery as a positive value which comes to be set in opposition to what remains merely problematic.

PAUL RICOEUR: But if the drama anticipates your philosophy, what happens to the autonomy of the philosophical act, of philosophical reflection? Could we accuse your philosophy of being a philosophy of the theater? You have insisted on the importance of what you call "secondary reflection." What place has the reflective moment in this meditation on drama and on the tragic in thinking?

GABRIEL MARCEL: I believe that the autonomy of the philosophical act, which is actually an act of reflection, must be recognized absolutely and safeguarded completely.

Moreover, I think you are right in recalling here what I have written about secondary reflection. What did I want to say exactly? I wanted to say that surely there is a primary reflection which, roughly speaking, is purely analytical and which consists, as it were, in dissolving the concrete into its elements.

But there is, I think, an inverse movement, a movement of retrieval, which consists in becoming aware of the partial and even suspect character of the purely analytical procedure. This reflective movement tries to reconstruct, but now at the level of thought, that concrete state of affairs which had previously been glimpsed in a fragmented or pulverized condition. It is quite certain that it is this secondary reflection which is at work in all my philosophical writings, starting from the moment when I truly became fully conscious of my task. Perhaps this is not yet sufficiently clear in the *Metaphysical Journal*. But it becomes perfectly clear in *Being and Having*, and even more so in the later writings.

PAUL RICOEUR: I am ready to concede the autonomy of philosophical reflection in your work, particularly because you never refer, or almost never, to your dramatic writings. Your philosophical reflection generally begins with examples, with situations, with concepts already elaborated which you then analyze. In this sense your philosophy finds and follows its own path.

GABRIEL MARCEL: Yes, I think that is absolutely correct. Moreover, I am happy you have spoken of the role of examples in my work. Actually, I believe this role is very important.

How many times have I said that thinking which does not deal seriously with examples always runs the risk of losing itself, of letting itself be deluded by a kind of antecedent linguistic structure? For me, giving an example is a way of justifying myself to myself, and also of proving to my interlocutor that I am speaking of something, that my words are not empty. I would almost say that examples serve as a kind of irrigation.

PAUL RICOEUR: Could we say that the philosophical example is like the dramatic character whose significance is not wholly revealed without some kind of existential confrontation?

GABRIEL MARCEL: Yes, but perhaps we should make this more precise by remarking that the character is like an embodied example. It is an example that enjoys a kind of autonomy and can thus be very stimulating philosophically. In this way the comparison is possible. Actually, what strikes me now after so many years is that I still find in my plays a kind of living interest or freshness which seems to be somewhat lacking in my philosophical writings to the extent that they are in some way too explicit, too summary, or have occasioned too many commentaries which are often mere repetitions rather than creative reflections. If I can make use of a histological comparison, I would say that drama for me is like living tissue; it is more capable of internal regeneration than is properly philosophical thinking. This, at least, is true for my own work. [TWB, pp. 230–236]

Chapter 7

On Other Philosophies

In the first selections, Marcel offers a scathing critique of Sartre's philosophy. He begins with a brief discussion of Sartre's famous "waiter" example, before turning to a penetrating critical analysis of several of Sartre's main themes, including his inadequate and deliberately distorted descriptions of various human experiences, such as sadness and gift-giving. Sartre always looks at the worst possible scenarios, according to Marcel, thereby missing the true experiences, and so his mis-descriptions are an act of sophistry. The same is true of Sartre's analysis of love. Marcel also offers a strong critique of Sartre's notions of freedom, his approach to the question of moral values, and of his atheism. He describes Sartre's overall approach as a nihilistic philosophy that can only lead to the vilification of man.

The next passage contains some reflections by Marcel on the thought of Martin Buber. Marcel is in agreement with Buber on several central themes, including the distinction between the I-Thou and I-It relation, the inadequacy of conceptual knowledge to describe human experience in its fullness, and the identification of the transcendent dimension of human existence. Here he comments on Buber's notion of relation, and on the notions of response and responsibility. He concludes with a brief analysis of the notion of existential guilt.

The third selection offers a brief critical reflection on Karl Jasper's view on religion.

We conclude with another conversation between Paul Ricoeur and Marcel. This is a wide-ranging discussion dealing with the relationship between Marcel's work and Christianity ("Christian existentialism"), as well as offering reflections on the work of various other existentialist philosophers, including Jaspers and Heidegger.

*   *   *

1. Marcel on Sartre

Now suppose that I am this waiter. I shall have to say that I am trying to achieve the being-in-itself of a waiter in a *cafe*. As though indeed it were not in my power to confer value and urgency upon my rights and duties of state; as though I were not at liberty to get up every morning at five or to stay in bed at the risk of being dismissed; as though, by the very fact of keeping up this role, I were not transcending it and, as it were, establishing a domain outside my condition as waiter. Yet it is beyond doubt that I am, in a sense, a waiter and not a diplomat or a journalist. But this cannot be true after the manner of being-in-itself, but only after the manner of being that which I am not; and this is true of every one of my attitudes and of my ways of behaving. Perpetually absent from my body and from my actions, I am, despite myself, that "divine absence" as it is termed by Valery. I cannot even say that I am here or that I am not here in the same sense as I say that this box of matches is, or is not, on this table.

This requires some elucidation. To go back a little: is the waiter a waiter by his essence, in the same way as he is, for instance, a male, born under such and such conditions? Evidently not. He is a waiter in the sense that *he has to be* a waiter, that he earns his living by fulfilling this role, and this is obviously true of many other kinds of function. Similarly, it is curious but profoundly true that I cannot say "I am here" or "I am not here" in the sense in which I say that this box is, or is not, on this table. I am here and yet I escape this mode of being on every side. I am, as it were, "in transit," as one who has just come and is about to leave. I am here because I have to be here and not by virtue of my essence.

But Sartre's analysis goes further still and it is here that it falls into sophistry:

> I "am" sad. But is not this sadness myself in the sense that I "am" what I am? Sadness is indeed the meaning of my mournful looks, of my hunched-up shoulders and of my bowed head. Yet, in the very act of assuming these postures, do I not know that I need not assume them? That, if a stranger came in suddenly, I would raise my head and change my expression; and what would be left of my sadness except the appointment I had made with it for a little later on, after my visitor has left? To be sad is to make oneself sad. . . . If I make myself sad I cannot be sad (in the sense in which a stone is heavy). The being of sadness escapes in and through the very act by which I assume it. The being-in-itself of

> *sadness haunts my consciousness of being sad, but only as an unattainable ideal; it is an indication of my sadness but not its constituent modality. (Being and Nothingness)*

I may be able to show the sophistry of this argument by an illustration to which the above passage rigorously applies. Suppose that I am going to the funeral of an acquaintance; I am sorry that he has died, but I am not moved at all deeply. Yet as I come into the house of mourning I am affected by its sadness. Indeed, I wish to some extent to be affected by it so as not to be out of tune with the bereaved family whom I have come to visit. I shall therefore not merely assume an outward deportment, saying to myself: "Now I must cast down my eyes and heave a deep sigh." I shall make a real effort (which indeed shows my natural bad faith) to think of the event as genuinely sad. I shall perhaps say to myself: "Poor gentleman, he might have lived another twenty years and enjoyed seeing his grandchildren," or "After all, he was not so much older than myself" or else "The same accident might have happened to Uncle So-and-so," so that by a kind of active goodwill I shall really succeed, as Sartre says, in feeling sad while knowing that in a moment, when I leave this house, I shall sigh with relief and dismiss my sadness like a cab.

All this is quite true, but just because it is true, it is easy to see that it is only part of the truth, and that to identify this kind of feeling with a genuine and profound grief can be only a bad joke. Note that there is a form of experience which, at least superficially, seems to bear out Sartre's view. Suppose that I am deeply grieved by the death of a friend and that someone calls on me who did not know my friend, and in whom I do not wish to confide. It may well be that I shall find in me the strength to control myself, and to appear to talk naturally about the weather or about politics. But does this mean that I have packed up my grief and deposited it like a parcel in the cloakroom? Not in the least; I remain profoundly grieved; sadness is still in the depth of my consciousness as something genuine and vivid which underlies the attitude I have adopted merely in order to conform to a social code. . . . [PE, pp. 64–67; essay originally published in 1946]

*   *   *

. . . Sartre, who is an extremely intelligent writer, saw that his play (*No Exit*) would be difficult to construct with irreproachable characters. However this may be, the play bears out what we have already observed in connection with "being seen" – the tendentiousness of Sartre's reasoning, which in the end becomes so marked that we are forced to ask ourselves what lies at the root of the prejudice which infects the whole of his work.

What, in fact, is Sartre's approach to the theory of the awareness of others? Its whole tendency is to assert that human communication is doomed to failure; that the sense of community – the sense of forming part of a *we*-subject is only experienced on such occasions as when a regiment is marching in step or a gang of workmen is pulling together, circumstances where the rhythm is in fact produced by myself and happens to coincide with that of the concrete community of which I am a member. But when it comes to the genuine community, the community of love or of friendship, Sartre's analysis of love in *L'Être et le Neant* and, still more the illustrations of that analysis in *L'Age de Raison*, reveal the fundamental agnosticism and even nihilism of his view.

Sartre's analysis of love is conducted in such a way that it is bound to arrive at a wholly negative conception. The aim of love is to appropriate the will of another, not for the sake of power, but in order to acquire absolute value in the eyes of the beloved, and thus to transform the alien gaze which had previously passed through me or had immobilized me in an in-itself.

The aim of love is to cease being seen as ugly or small or cowardly; instead of feeling that my existence is superfluous I would feel that it is upheld and willed, even in its smallest details, by an absolute will, an absolute "freedom," which is itself conditioned by my own existence and willed by my own freedom. The essence of the joy of love, in so far as it exists, is to feel that my existence is justified. As will be remembered, existence was represented as the awareness of superfluity. But now, through the miracle of successful love (in the improbable event that love can ever be successful) the sense of superfluity would be replaced by the sense that my existence is justified, that it is, as it were, snatched out of the orbit of that ultimate contingency which is, as we have seen, the fundamental principle of *La Nausée*.

But it must be said at once that this ideal is regarded as utterly unattainable. Sartre shows to what perversions, to what extremes of sadism or masochism love can give rise when it does not sink into indifference or degenerate into hate. Incidentally, each of these by-products carries with it a duality which tends to dissolve it. It would be too long to go into details, but an important point is that the death of the beloved does not resolve the problem in any sense. That which I was for the other is perpetuated by the other's death; I am that irremediably in the past, and also in the present and the future to the extent that I keep to the attitudes, the plans, the way of life, which the other has judged. The death of the other constitutes me irremediably as a thing, in exactly the same way as would happen through my own death. This is why the death of Xaviere in *L'Invitée*, by Simone de Beauvoir, resolves absolutely nothing. On the contrary, the triumph of Xaviere is perpetuated by the very fact that she is killed by Françoise.

It is clear that the whole of this dialectic, with its undeniable power and agility, rests upon the complete denial of *we* as subject, that is to say upon the denial of communion. For Sartre this word has no meaning at any possible level, not to speak of its religious or mystical sense. This is because in his universe, participation itself is impossible: this, philosophically, is the essential point. There is room only for appropriation, and this in a domain where appropriation is impracticable or where, if it is achieved, it fails of its object. Take, for instance, the case of a man who succeeds in enslaving his wife. She becomes his instrument, his thing; he can do with her what he wills. But the probable result is that this successful appropriation will destroy his love for her. She will lose all interest for him and the climax of success will prove to be the climax of failure. This truth has been seen long before Sartre; its inexorable logic cannot be escaped except by recognizing that the aim of love is quite different from appropriation, that it is a communion the nature of which must be understood before the cause of the failure can be grasped.

We must now turn our attention to that "freedom" of which Sartre constantly speaks and ask ourselves in what it consists. Sartre claims in conversation that he is the only man who today can speak of the absolute because for him freedom has the value of an absolute; I can think of nothing more preposterous. What then is this freedom? His definitions of it are obscure. We must not be put off by such formulae as that freedom is man's faculty to secrete his own non-being, or that it is man's capacity to be the foundation of himself; as in the case of existence, we must refer to his actual experience of freedom as he describes it, particularly in *Le Sursis*. [PE, pp. 74–77]

*   *   *

. . . [The words] "I am condemned to freedom" should be underlined. What would that have sounded like, say, to a Descartes or to a Biran or to any other genuine philosopher of the past? Surely as a most regrettable *flatus vaci*. To what indeed can I be condemned? Surely it must be to a loss, to a deprivation – whether of life, of wealth, of honor or of freedom. I cannot be "condemned" to freedom unless freedom is a deprivation, a loss. And indeed, for Sartre freedom is, like consciousness, a deprivation, a defect; it is only by a kind of paralogism that he later represents this defect as the positive condition of the emergence of a world and thus bestows upon it a creative value.

. . . I do not believe that in the whole history of human thought, grace, even in its most secularized forms, has ever been denied with such audacity or such impudence. Having taken this step, Sartre naturally finds himself under the necessity to establish that every human action, even when it appears to be determined, is in reality free – that is to say, the result of choice. Note that for him freedom is equivalent to choice (1 believe this to be a fatal error). His ideas on this subject can be summed up in a few simple propositions:

1. Being, in the case of human beings, is equivalent to doing. Man reveals himself, under observation, as an organized unit of behaviors and comportments.
2. But the characteristic of this manner of being is its self-determination: the existence of an act postulates its autonomy (not, of course, in the Kantian meaning of this term).
3. The nature of an act is defined by its intention, and this intention always goes beyond the given actuality in its tension towards a result to be achieved – that is to say, towards a chosen end.
4. It is this end which reveals the nature of the world, and the world reveals itself for what it is in accordance with the nature of the chosen end.
5. Intention, which does not arise *out* of the given actuality but *away from* it, makes a break with what is given. This break is necessary for the awareness of what is given to be possible; it is through this that what is given can become a motivating force. It can even be said that the break is what makes the given actuality by shedding upon it the light of what does not exist as yet, that is to say of the proposed end.
6. If consciousness starts from actuality, it is only by denying it, by disengaging itself from something which already exists, to engage in the struggle for what does not exist as yet. This characteristic of being-in-itself postulates that this kind of being finds no support or assistance in its own past. Thus, not only do we not inherit anything from others, but we do not even inherit anything from ourselves. We can never be aware of ourselves as anything but a choice which is in process of being made. Now, freedom consists simply in this fact that the choice is always unconditional.

7. Incidentally, the choice is always absurd, since it is beyond all reasons, and since it is impossible not to choose.
8. Lastly, a free intention, a free initial project is fundamental to my being; indeed it is my being itself. There exists in every one of us an initial project, which can he laid bare by the appropriate phenomenological method of existential psychoanalysis.

These propositions should really be discussed and illustrated in detail, but I must confine myself to a criticism of the most important points.

To begin with, I am inclined to think that, as on so many occasions, Sartre makes an exaggerated use of the concept of negation. "To disengage oneself from" is not the same thing as to "deny," and the term *néantisation* is highly equivocal. Let us take any one of innumerable examples. Say that a man who feels that his family life has too tight a hold on him, that he has been too cosseted and too spoilt, seeks to disengage himself from his family. This is not at all the same thing as saying that he "denies" his family. It may simply mean that he is trying to establish a free relationship in place of what had been a stranglehold. This simple example taken from everyday life shows how unsuitable and even dishonest – I can find no other word for it – is the use of the term *néantisation* with its deliberately negative associations. But there is something still more serious.

Can it be legitimate to say that, for the human being, being is equivalent to doing? Is this not something more than a simplification? Is it not a misapprehension of what is deepest and most significant in the nature of man? How can it be right to ignore the distinction, commonly made, between what a man is and what he does? Does not this statement alone reveal the inadequacy of Sartre's ontology?

And, on the other hand, is it not plainly contrary to experience to assert that being-for-itself finds no support in its own past? Here we come back once more to the infinitely weighty question raised by what I have described as Sartre's rejection of grace in whatever form. Anybody less capable than Sartre of understanding the significance of receiving or the nature of gift cannot be conceived; it is sufficient to recall his astonishingly distorted analysis of generosity: "To give is to appropriate by means of destroying and to use this act of destruction as a means of enslaving others." Gift is a means of enslaving others through the destruction of a certain object; not that this object is broken, but that it is destroyed in so far as it ceases to be mine. Does such a definition convey any genuine experience of giving? No doubt, if I had sufficient space, I could show, as in connection with sadness, that there are extreme cases to which this analysis applies, cases in which giving is used as a means of enslaving. But it is clearly impossible to generalize from this to the universal nature of giving without falling into absurdity and even into scandalous abuse.

What it comes to is this (and it is an attitude which seems to me to lay bare the roots of metaphysical pride): for Sartre, to receive is incompatible with being free; indeed, a being who is free is bound to deny to himself that he has received anything. But I wonder if here the author of *La Nausée* does not fall into one of the worst errors which can be attributed to Idealism. Granted the many qualifications to which any statement on the history of philosophy must be subject, it is true to say that because Kant and some of his followers conceived the spirit in terms of constructive activity, they tended to make a confusion between receiving and suffering and to ascribe receptivity exclusively to matter. This is another illustration of the misleading role played by material images. As soon as the one who receives is conceived as a "recipient," the true character of receptivity is ignored. As soon as receptivity in a spiritual, or even in a living, being is confused with suffering in a material sense (in the sense in which wax suffers the imprint of a seal) it becomes impossible to conceive the concrete and organic relationship between the individual and the world. There remain only two terms of reference: an actuality which is, so to speak, inert, and a freedom which denies it only to assume it in an incomprehensible way at a later stage.

What is, at any rate, certain is that, in such a philosophy, the notion of freedom, be it even as non-being or, to use a concrete image, as an air-pocket in the midst of being-in-itself, is just as inexplicable and much more deeply unintelligible than the notion of creation which Sartre rejects and for which he has nothing but contempt. The truth is that Sartre unites the idealism of which I have spoken with a materialism which derives from the eighteenth-century tradition of French thought. Indeed, I have heard recently that one of his disciples, lecturing at Lyons, admitted this filiation and claimed this double authority in support of Sartre's teaching. But this admission brings us to a curious paradox. Existentialism (I have surely not abused this word) has developed historically as a reaction against the Hegelian system; yet it is now seen to emerge – like the tunnels on the St. Gothard railway – considerably *below* the level from which it had started. Clearly, from the standpoint of Hegel himself, the concept of being-in-itself is to be found at a very low level of dialectics. And Sartre himself constantly asserts that man is a useless passion, or that he vainly aspires to achieve in his own person the impossible synthesis which would result in being-in-itself.

Man's life is an attempt, continually renewed and inevitably doomed to failure, at the divinisation of himself.

Note that this is not without truth. It is true that man seems to be irresistibly urged to confer upon himself the attributes of divinity, and the progress of technics lends a disquieting semblance of truth to the tempter's promise: *eritis sicut dii*. But the existence and the danger of this temptation are recognized the more easily the more firmly are asserted the existence and the transcendence of God. Whereas here we are, on the contrary, in the presence of explicit and aggressive atheism. It is no exaggeration to say this, for Sartre himself recently stated in conversation that his atheism was becoming increasingly militant and aggressive. There are to be found in *L'Être et le Néant* certain rudimentary proofs of the non-existence of God which show the depth and persistence of the author's rationalism; indeed, it is perhaps by means of this very acid that his philosophy corrodes the contemporary mind. As I have mentioned earlier, it even happens to him to reason in the manner of a Bernardin de St. Pierre *a rebours*, as when he argues from certain biological phenomena of inadaptation or of teleological incoherence to the fundamental absurdity of the universe or to the non-existence of God.

But perhaps we should recall at this point the assertion made by Sartre himself of the existence in each of us of an initial pattern which existential psychoanalysis should he able to reveal. Should we not ask what is the pattern at the origin of Sartre's atheism? The answer can be only one of two things. Either he must admit that his atheism derives from an attitude of the will or from an initial resentment (as would be the case of a man who, from the very depth of his being, willed that God should not exist); such an answer would be in keeping with his doctrine, but it would destroy much of its metaphysical bearing. Or else he must take up his stand on the traditional ground of objective thought and declare that *there is no God*, as one might say that there are no people on Mars; but in that case he must give up the plane of existentialism and fall back on the most obsolete positions of traditional rationalism.

This metaphysical aspect of the problem raised by Sartre's philosophy is not, however, the one with which this paper is intended to deal. The essential question is, to my mind, whether this philosophy is not heading for the abyss into which the forces of self-destruction threaten to drive our unfortunate race. For my part, I am convinced of it and this is the crucial point on which I must insist in conclusion.

I have recently surprised and even scandalized some of Sartre's followers by classifying his philosophy among the "techniques of vilification," by which I mean techniques which result, whether deliberately or not, in the systematic vilification of man. I admit that, superficially, this would seem to be a paradox, for does not Sartre ceaselessly exalt man and his freedom in the face of the radical absurdity of the universe? But it must not be forgotten that the Fascist dictatorships, whether in Germany, Italy or elsewhere, similarly exalted "the people" and offered it a ceaseless and cheap adulation; yet what contempt did not this adulation conceal, and to what abject depth did they not reduce their citizens. I greatly fear that the relationship between Sartre and his disciples on the one hand and between them and the humanity they claim to exalt on the other may follow an analogous pattern. Etymologically, to vilify a thing is to take away its value, its price. This can be done in the case of merchandise by flooding the market, and this is just what Sartre does to freedom: he debases it by putting it on every stall. "If freedom were easy, everything would fall to pieces at once," says Pierre Bost in his remarkable recent short story, *Monsieur l'Amiral va bientôt mourir.* No doubt, Sartre would indignantly protest against the suggestion that, in his philosophy, freedom is easy. But in that case he can surely not maintain the statement which he makes in *L'Être et le Néant* and again in *Les Chemins de la Liberté*, that "we are condemned to be free." If we are condemned to be free, then freedom must be easy. It is true that a distinction can be made between freedom and the use of freedom, but this is out of keeping with the doctrine; for we must not forget that Sartre does not regard it as an instrument which is at the disposal of man and of which he can consequently make a good or a bad use; he regards it as man's very being or his lack of being.

So that it is only by a kind of sleight of hand that this freedom which man is and which he cannot help being, can be later converted into a freedom which he owns and of which he can make a wrong use.

This raises the whole question of values as they are conceived by Sartre. From his standpoint, values cannot be anything but the result of the initial choice made by each human being; in other words, they can never be "recognized" or "discovered." "My freedom," he states expressly, "is the unique foundation of values. And since I am the being by virtue of whom values exist, nothing – absolutely nothing – can justify me in adopting this or that value or scale of values. As the unique basis of the existence or values, I am totally unjustifiable. And my freedom is in anguish at finding that it is the baseless basis of values." Nothing could be more explicit; but the question is whether Sartre does not here go counter to the exigencies of that human reality which he claims, after all, not to invent but to reveal.

Not to deal exclusively in abstractions, let us take a concrete case. Sartre has announced that the third volume of his *Les Chemins de la Liberté* is to be devoted to the praise of the heroes of Resistance. Now I ask you in the name of what principle, having first denied the existence of values or at least of their objective basis, can he establish any appreciable difference between those utterly misguided but undoubtedly courageous men who joined voluntarily the Anti-Bolshevik Legion, on the one hand, and the heroes of the Resistance movement, on the other? I can see no way of establishing this difference without admitting that causes have their intrinsic value and, consequently, that values are real. I have no doubt that Sartre's ingenuity will find a way out of this dilemma; in fact, he quite often uses the words "good" and "bad," but what can these words possibly mean in the context of his philosophy?

The truth is that, if I examine myself honestly and without reference to any preconceived body of ideas, I find that I do not "choose" my values at all, but that I *recognize* them and then posit my actions in accordance or in contradiction with these values, not, however, without being painfully aware of this contradiction (as was clear to the ancients: *video meliora proboque, deteriora sequor*). It should perhaps be asked at this point if it is not Nietzsche who, with his theory of the creation of values, is responsible for the deathly principle of error which has crept into speculation on this subject. But although I am the last to underrate the objections to Nietzsche's doctrine, I am inclined to think that his view is less untenable than that of Sartre, for it escapes that depth of rationalism and materialism which is discernible, to me as to others, in the mind of the author of *L'Être et le Néant*.

I would suggest in conclusion that existentialism stands today at a parting of the ways: it is, in the last analysis, obliged either to deny or to transcend itself. It denies itself quite simply when it falls to the level of infra-dialectical materialism. It transcends itself, or it tends to transcend itself, when it opens itself out to the experience of the suprahuman, an experience which can hardly be ours in a genuine and lasting way this side of death, but of which the reality is attested by mystics, and of which the possibility is warranted by any philosophy which refuses to be immured in the postulate of absolute immanence or to subscribe in advance to the denial of the beyond and of the unique and veritable transcendence. Not that there is anything in this which, in our itinerant condition, we can invest like a capital; this absolute life can be apprehended by us only in flashes and by virtue of a hidden initiative which can be nothing other than grace. I am, of course, thinking of the extravagantly dogmatic negativism which is common to Sartre, to Heidegger and even to Jaspers. It is true that Sartre has criticized with some force the notion of being-for-death which dominates the thought of Heidegger; but it is all too clear that there is little to choose between that view and his own, which is equally opaque. I cannot help stating once more in this connection the dilemma to which I referred earlier on: either this assertion of man's total mortality is the expression of an existential wish – and in that case it cannot be other than contingent – or else it presupposes an objective, pseudo-scientific realism in regard to death, and implies a crass materialism which belongs to the infraexistential levels of philosophy.

Sartre verbally admits this materialism: "What will you," he says, "matter is the only reality I am able to grasp. " Yet I am persuaded that this negative realism, this way of cramping the spirit to the experience of the senses, while relating this experience whenever possible to behaviorist illustrations, cannot go without a corresponding devaluation of the truly human modes of existence. In this connection, I declare without hesitation, and at the risk of bringing down on myself the thunderbolts of his partisans, that it is by no means a coincidence if Sartre's work offers the most glaring display of obscenities to be found in the whole of contemporary art. It is no use talking to me of Celine – I have far too much respect for Sartre to compare him with his wretched predecessor; nor should he be compared with Zola, who was, after all, only a healthy, naive "naturalist," not at all a philosopher and not blessed with too much intelligence. Given that in Sartre's world man's inherence in the universe is ignored or denied and that its level is therefore infinitely below the pantheism of the Stoics or of Spinoza, it is not at all surprising that in it man should conceive of himself more and more as waste matter or as potential excrement. Whatever the third volume of *Les Chemins de la Liberté* is like, whatever the paper garlands that Sartre picks from the literature of the *maquis* to put on his heroes' tombs, I cannot see that the substance of his doctrine is likely to alter. For such a change to be effective and not merely to be one of lighting or decor, the very principles of his philosophy would have to be revised; and nothing leads us at present to foresee the likelihood of such a revision.

And indeed we must admit that it would be an almost unheard of thing for a philosopher who has achieved his degree of notoriety and who is, if not intoxicated with success (he is too intelligent for that), at least fully engaged in pressing his advantages simultaneously in every field, to put forth the heroic effort (for it would be nothing less than that) required for a serious reconsideration of postulates which find a deep echo in his nature and, so to speak, in his psychic make-up. Everything suggests, on the contrary, that his views will harden still further. The only question is whether, at a given moment, he will not move closer to Marxism, not that the Marxists, who are ill-disposed towards him, are likely to welcome him into their ranks. This will become clear in the near future. Meanwhile, it is from the ranks of a misdirected and anarchical youth that he will, either directly or through his zealous intermediaries, recruit his disciples and, so often, his victims. [PE, pp. 79–90]

*   *   *

2. Marcel on Buber

I feel tempted to put forward a small objection against Buber concerning the term "relation"; to my mind this term is suffused with generality and, what is more, it implies a concept, that is to say, objectivated data. We can probably best understand what is involved and meant here if we recall an actual encounter that was experienced as such. And let us not forget how difficult it is to find adequate terminology in this area! For example, when Buber uses the word "vis-à-vis" he does not, it seems to me, point up sufficiently the difference between what he wishes to capture in the term and "opposition" in the true sense. Yet I have to admit it is quite difficult to make the necessary distinction between the elements of "opposition" and of "co-presence on the scene." But I feel that some of the texts we cited sufficiently show how Buber manages to catch our attention and stir us to such a degree that we feel obliged to respond.

In this kind of philosophy the concept of response is as central as that of responsibility. There can only be authentic responsibility where there is a genuine response. But response to what? "Every given hour with its contents of world and destiny is a personal message to whoever is attentive; being attentive is all that is required to start reading the signs one receives."

We might already guess at this point that the machinery of our civilization intervenes to obstruct or even stop this constant flow of messages. Conscience, on the other hand, consciousness in the moral and ethical sense of the word, is receptivity to these messages. And on this point Buber obviously differs with Heidegger. For the author of *Sein und Zeit* (Being and Time) "existence is a monologue." The man of authentic existence in Heidegger's mind is not the man who truly lives with other people, but rather a man "who knows true life only in dealing *with himself.*"

We must return once more to the vexing question: Who speaks to us? Buber's answer seems to be of decisive importance. We must not reply: God – "unless we say it from the perspective of that deciding hour of personal existence when we had to forget everything that was handed down to us, learned, self-devised, every bit of book knowledge, and were immersed into obscure night." Buber uses the following comparison: To anyone who really wants to absorb a poem, biographical data about the poet are of no use; the "I" that he faces is the subject, the "I" of this particular, singular poem. The situation is entirely different when we want to get an idea about a particular poet by reading a number of his poems.

I would personally go even further than Buber; I would ask whether the question "who" should not be eliminated entirely. For the question aims ultimately at an identification that is only possible in the objective world, or where it is possible to establish certain criteria. (I have the identification in mind which police commissars are after.) But in our case the question is not: Is it he? but rather and explicitly: Is it you? The act by which I declare: "Yes, this is you," is beyond the possibility of an identification, because identification refers to a specific thing among other things. And it is precisely this "among others" that is impossible because of the singularity of the "Thou."

This is probably what Buber means anyway when he emphasizes the necessity of "holding on to God," as he puts it. He explains clearly that what one has to hold on to is not an image of God, or a concept one has of God, but God as being. He uses another comparison: The earth depends on the sun as existing, and not as some concept that the earth might conceivably have of the sun.

Evidently what is meant here by the term "holding on to" is faith in its specific sense.

In the introduction to the important treatise *Zwei Glaubensweisen* (Two Kinds of Faith) Buber stresses the difference which exists in his opinion between thinking as a rational function of the mind and faith in the proper sense. Rational thinking constitutes only a part or a partial function of my being. But when I believe "my whole being, my being in its totality, enters into the process; in fact, the process only becomes possible by virtue of the fact that my relation of faith is a relation of my whole being. Personal totality in this sense, however, can only be accomplished if the entire function of thinking is also integrated into the totality without impairment and is permitted to operate as subordinate to and determined by it."

We want to make sure at this point that there is no question of replacing the term "totality" with the term "feeling." Feeling is no way the whole; at best it is an indication that the being of man "is about to unite into a totality." But I am not quite sure that I understand exactly what Buber means here by the phrase "is about." In the main, however, his thought is clear, and it would certainly be a grave mistake to classify it as irrational. Buber, for example, wants to point out that confidence in the strict sense does not rest on any motives. Motives rather offer themselves in retrospect to the justifying consciousness. This does not make Buber's thinking irrational. For him, reason, if merged with the spirit, infinitely surpasses analytical and calculating reasoning. (S, pp. 84–86)

*   *   *

Before I conclude, I want to make a few observations on Buber's interpretation of guilt and guilt feelings.

Our author takes, as we will see presently, a very strong position against the temptation to which so many psychoanalysts and sociologists succumb; the temptation is to dissolve guilt as such into nothingness and to analyze only in what way guilt is felt or accepted. Buber is concerned with exploring guilt insofar as it is more than merely a psychological reaction or a taboo still existing in the depths of the unconscious.

Let us take a man who has burdened his conscience by acting in a certain way under exactly determined circumstances, or he may, on the contrary, have defaulted by omission, or he was a party to what might appear to him a collective guilt. After years he is still haunted by a sense of guilt. He is aware of the minute details of the evil he has perpetrated and is unable to keep his mind off them.

> *That which keeps attacking him has nothing whatsoever to do with a parental or societal censure, and if he has no retribution to fear from the temporal powers and does not believe in a retribution in the hereafter, there is no threat of punishment to scare him. What comes into play here is the penetrating insight that we cannot return to the point of departure and that what is done is irreparable; that is, the real insight into the irreversibility of time spent, a fact which is most inescapable in the perspective of one's own death, the strongest of all human perspectives. From no point is time more felt as fall than from the point of the guilty man's view of himself. Tumbling downward in this fall, the guilty party is visited by the horrors of being identical with himself. I, he is given to understand, who have changed, am still the same.*

Existential guilt, that is the guilt with which a person as such has burdened himself, cannot be handled by such categories of analysis as repression or making-conscious. The guilty party is fully aware of the action he regrets. To be sure, he frequently tries to push this aside, but what is being pushed away is not the fact as such but its existential depth. The order of the world of man has been violated, and the guilty one knows and recognizes this order fully. This idea of order is of fundamental significance and precludes any possibility of a merely subjective interpretation. This explains why Buber categorically opposes the escape device to which Aldous Huxley, for example, resorts when he recommends the use of mescaline.

I would only like to point here to a certain terminological inconsistency when our philosopher speaks of the "objective relationship which two people have with one another." The use of the word "objective" seems objectionable to me, as it involves the danger of our being led back to a way of thinking that could be termed "preexistential." There is danger of confusing objectivity with actuality, something that can very easily happen. The deep meaning, however, is beyond any doubt. Buber is always concerned with awakening us to the awareness of interhuman relationships. The principal merit of Buber is to have focused the limelight on the structural rather than the formal conditions that are vital for humanity; if these conditions are not heeded it might well be that mankind degenerates right before our very eyes.

I would have liked to show in more detail how Buber throughout his life and with admirable persistence has made every effort to concretize his thought and put it into flesh and blood. I want to give at least one example that I feel is extremely typical. I have in mind the attitude Buber took in the Palestine conflict and which exposed him to attacks from various quarters. He spoke out resolutely against the nationalism that inflamed the two communities against each other. He would have wanted very much to bring about some sort of coexistence, a *convivencia* between the two nations which, with the religious differences remaining intact, would have led them to respect one another. Buber was able to look beyond the present conditions and the aroused passions, whereas neither of the two communities could. In this Buber was the leader on a path whose end is still obscured by night.

I am the first to admit that this lecture only outlines a very small sector of Buber's thought. It would give me satisfaction, however, if my inadequate observations were to stir in some of you the desire to get in direct contact with his work. There is no special jargon in Buber; on the contrary, his writings are distinguished by a clarity seldom found in contemporary writers. I hardly have to mention that it is Buber's constant preoccupation with the other person that sets his thinking apart. The *other person* is not primarily a threat, as he is for Sartre, but rather a brother whom I must try to understand and on whom I can lean and rely even if I feel I have to oppose him. [S, pp. 90–92]

*   *   *

3. Marcel on Jaspers

. . . Jasper's conclusions, whatever else they may be, seem to represent an attempt, or at any rate one he imagined he was making, to overcome both positivism and idealism, an attempt which is marked in places by the doctrines against which the author is struggling and which he claims to transcend. In the course of my discussion I have indicated the contempt he displays for all conceptions of immortality; does he not affirm that it is mortality, on the contrary, that can be demonstrated? And we must not be misled in this respect, for what we have here after all is a psycho-physiological dogmatism. To be sure, it must be acknowledged that within the framework of this dogmatism of the here-below, he makes an heroic effort to elevate himself as high as possible to the transcendent. But how evade the fact that he moves within a certain *enclosed space*? It is useless to be told that this space has no assignable boundaries, for this only makes it still more bounded, even confined. And without realizing it, he forces us in the final analysis to ask whether he is not simply effecting an unjustified secularization of certain essentially religious ideas whose vital springs, however, have already been broken. I am thinking here, in particular, of his notion of guilt. Jaspers uses the word *Schuld* in this context, and not *Sunde;* but how to ignore the fact that this ineradicable guilt which is coessential with us, represents the trace or abstract vestige of original sin? I make these observations with a certain timidity because I have not subjected Jasper's thought to a thorough examination; but it seems to me that the manner in which he presents his religious philosophy directly confirms my remarks. Doesn't he actually finish by telling us that everyone should remain in the religious faith in which he has been brought up – because it is a part of his fundamental situation – but that he cannot escape the fact that he will most certainly cut the figure of a heretic within the religious faith of his upbringing; and doesn't he refer to the spontaneous tendency of philosophy towards heresy? This point seems to me extremely significant. Jasper's position with respect to existence necessarily tends to make him reject any idea of religious canonicity or orthodoxy, and this is only an expression on the religious level of a radical rejection of the ontological as such. We have here reached the central point of his doctrine, the point at which I shall conclude my remarks. I believe that if we sanction this rejection, it would not be easy to find a body of thought today which is more profound, more supple and more hospitable to the mind, than Jasper's. I also believe that if we proclaim his doctrine to be a fundamental perversion of reason, we shall be led to revise all of Jasper's positions and to add another dimension to his thought whereby it becomes completely transfigured. [CF, pp. 253–254]

*   *   *

4. A conversation between Paul Ricoeur and Gabriel Marcel

PAUL RICOEUR: In this fourth conversation, M. Marcel, I want to ask a question we cannot put off any longer. A tag – there's no other word for it – has been attached to your work, the tag of Christian existentialism. People like to say that there is an atheistic existentialism, that of Sartre and Heidegger, and a Christian existentialism, that of Jaspers and Gabriel Marcel. What do you think about this?

GABRIEL MARCEL: I must say that I'm completely against this classification. You know as well as I do that Sartre was the one who started it in his well-known lecture on existentialism as a humanism. I cannot protest enough against this way of putting the matter. In fact I have never spontaneously used the word "existentialism." It was in 1946 at the Rome Congress that I found out that someone had used the word to characterize my work. At the time I was rather unconcerned. But shortly afterward I did become concerned when someone came to ask whether I would agree to the title *Christian Existentialism* for a commemorative volume which was to be dedicated to me in the collection *Presence* which Plan publishes.

I have to say that on the whole I did not find the idea very agreeable. I made it a point nevertheless to ask the advice of a man I had a great deal of confidence in, Louis Lavelle. I said to him: "You know my work. I have a great deal of confidence in your judgment. What do you think of the matter?" He answered: "I understand very well that you don't like the phrase 'Christian existentialism.' I don't like it either. It seems to me nonetheless that you can make a concession to your publisher." So I yielded. But very soon when I became aware of the inanities the word "existentialism" led to, and especially among society women, I was sorry to have been so accommodating. Since 1949 I've said on every occasion that I reject this tag, and more generally that I'm repelled by labels and "isms."

PAUL R1COEUR: Nevertheless, that summary characterization included an adjective, the adjective "Christian." We can't get away without some discussion on this point.

GABRIEL MARCEL: Certainly not.

PAUL R1COEUR: How do you see the relationship of your philosophy to Christianity? I'm asking the question because, without any ill will, someone might object to your thinking along these lines. When you speak of the ontological mystery, you are using a word taken from the language of Christianity, the word "mystery." But the word "ontological" belongs to the language of philosophy. Doesn't the expression "ontological mystery" really say *too* much for the philosopher, and not enough for the believer or at least for the theologian, inasmuch as you make no specific reference to the person of Christ as such? What do you think of this line of reasoning?

GABRIEL MARCEL: Here we have to go back quite a bit. What has to be seen is how I came to Christianity. You know I was raised without any religion and that, nevertheless, from the moment I began to think philosophically for myself, it seemed I was irresistibly drawn to think favorably of Christianity. That is, I was drawn to recognize that there must be an extremely profound reality in Christianity and that my duty as a philosopher was to find out how this reality could be understood. The problem I had then was truly a problem of intelligibility. That was when I used to hand in my writings to Victor Delbos, and I used to feel what a great interest he had in this inquiry. But over the years I found myself in the quite unusual situation of someone who believed deeply in the faith of others and who was completely convinced that this faith was *not* illusory, yet who could not acknowledge the possibility or the right of taking this faith absolutely on its own account. There was a paradox there – I saw this very clearly – which lasted a long time. I might also say that I walked a tight rope for a long time, and that at a certain moment I needed some outside intervention, that of Mauriac, to help me face this anomaly, to question, to ask myself: "Do I really have the right to stay any longer on this path?" No, I felt drawn to profess my allegiance openly. This happened at a time in my life when I was at peace with myself and when there was no special anxiety. For me this was a reason for thinking that the invitation Mauriac addressed to me should be taken absolutely seriously. I have probably told you that I hesitated for some moments. I said to myself: "I must become a Christian, I must enter a church, but will this be the reformed church?" My wife was Protestant and we were extraordinarily close. I have the greatest affection for her family. I have a brother-in-law who is a minister and who is really like a confidant to me. But I chose Catholicism. The influence of du Bos was certainly the major one. It seemed to me that choosing Christianity meant choosing Christianity in its fullness, and that I would find this fullness more in Catholicism than in Protestantism. It seemed to me that Protestantism offered only partial, variable, and sometimes inconsistent expressions of this fullness, and that it would be very difficult to choose among these expressions. That's exactly how things happened.

You referred to that essential text on the ontological mystery which came after my conversion. My conversion was in 1929 and that text was written in 1932. I don't believe it is easy to specify exactly what the relationship was between this kind of experience – I can use the word properly here – this lived experience which accompanied and followed my conversion, and what is said in this text. I believe that even at the time I was writing those reflections on the ontological mystery I experienced the need to reach a level universal enough to make what I was saying acceptable or understandable by non-Catholics and even perhaps by non-Christians, so long as they had a certain apprehension of what seemed to me essential.

PAUL RICOEUR: You speak somewhere about the peri-Christian zones of existence. It's these you wanted to touch on in your work. But the question remains. When you take up the themes of hope and fidelity, aren't you exploring theological dimensions?

GABRIEL MARCEL: Of course. . . .

PAUL RICOEUR: You refused the title "Christian existentialist." But if the bond between "I believe" and "I exist" is constitutive of your philosophy, if it contains the principle for every refutation of despair, don't you have to accept the term "Christian philosophy"?

GABRIEL MARCEL: Strictly speaking yes . . . perhaps I would accept this term to the extent that I reject the position Brehier took when he denied – which seems completely absurd to me – that life or Christian experience could include elements capable of nourishing and enriching philosophical thought. In this way, that is, as a negation of a negation, I would accept the idea of a Christian philosophy. But let us return to what you were just saying, something which is very important. I consider myself as having always been a philosopher of the threshold, a philosopher who kept himself in rather uncomfortable fashion on a line midway between believers and nonbelievers so that he could somehow stand with believers, with the Christian religion, the Catholic religion, but also speak to nonbelievers, make himself understood by them and perhaps to help them. I don't think this kind of preoccupation is an apologetic one – that word would be completely inappropriate – but I do think that this fraternal concern has played an extremely important role in the development of my thought. Thus the questions or objections you've brought up are certainly legitimate, and I am not dismissing them. But I must somehow specify and locate the place where I have always stood, where perhaps I continue to stand. . . .

PAUL RICOEUR: This threshold position links you with Jaspers and Heidegger. I would very much like to discuss this with you.

GABRIEL MARCEL: Certainly.

PAUL RICOEUR: I am letting myself draw you onto this ground because some years ago when I wrote about you I was myself much more aware of your kinship with Jaspers than with Heidegger. But today I think I would emphasize the distance and even the opposition I've since noticed between you and Jaspers, and on the other hand I would underline everything which, despite very strong appearances to the contrary, draws you closer to Heidegger.

GABRIEL MARCEL: I think you're completely right. It's certain that when I read Jaspers's *Philosophy* – that must have been in 1933 if I'm not mistaken – I was extremely impressed. In many ways this reading seemed liberating. I am alluding especially to volume two, *Existence*. I found there masterly analyses, particularly of what Jaspers calls limit situations, and you remember that I wrote a study then which first appeared in the *Recherches philosophiques* and which afterwards was included in the book *Creative Fidelity*. I was attracted much less by volume three, *Transcendence*. It seemed to me that there the idea of cipher which

Jaspers used so copiously remained equivocal. It was impossible to get a firm grip on it.

PAUL RICOEUR: My own tendency would be to view Jaspers's second volume with the same reservations you just mentioned. His philosophy of freedom stresses choice so much, that is, self-choice in anxiety, whereas I see a more Claudellian strain in your philosophy of freedom. For you, the freedom of response goes beyond the freedom of choice. By way of contrast I am much more aware now that in Jaspers's philosophy of freedom the major emphasis is on exile, solitude, and refusal. This is what moves all his thought toward a kind of romantic speculation on failure, something that runs throughout his thought. I'm thinking of texts like the doctrine of the night in which everything that has an order must be destroyed, where the night is seen as the thrust of existence toward its own ruin. I don't think that you could have written that kind of text.

GABRIEL MARCEL: Certainly not. Romantic and, if I remember well enough, Wagnerian strains can be detected in his philosophy, don't you think? No, I think you're completely right.

PAUL RICOEUR: What place does the theme of anxiety have in your philosophy?

GABRIEL MARCEL: Yes, this question has to be met head-on. Certainly for me the theme of anxiety is not the central theme of what I would call, *grosso modo*, my philosophy of existence. Perhaps this is what makes a very great difference between myself and, for example, Heidegger. It has become more and more clear to me – and here in fact we meet Claudel again – that there could be an existential experience of joy and of fullness. And I believe also that what you pointed out about freedom is perfectly correct. The identification of freedom with freedom of choice was a mistake. Just this morning I had to make a somewhat painful decision. It was a matter of my recalling from a publisher a certain text that he had asked me for, because I realized that if this text were published it would put someone else in danger. I didn't hesitate. I said: "The text has to be recalled, even suppressed." I had made no real choice there, and yet I had never felt more free than at that moment. Why? Because there was nothing resembling an outside necessity. There was just this certainty that I would be betraying myself, be wanting in my own person, be putting myself in contradiction with everything I had always thought and said yes to, if I failed to recall the text and as a result exposed someone else to serious danger. This example seems to me quite revealing.

PAUL RICOEUR: I want to come back to the theme of anxiety because it has been a source of misunderstanding between Heidegger and you. Heidegger's texts on anxiety have too often been read by way of Sartre. Actually, for Heidegger the anxiety provoked by the contingency of everything is the result of a disengagement from what you would call the ontological dimension. This brings me back to the suggestion I just made, that perhaps you are very close to Jaspers in appearance, but under the surface very close to Heidegger. What Heidegger calls the forgetfulness of being has an echo in your analysis of having, of *indisponibilité* [lack of openness, availability] and of despair. Similarly your use of questioning, which we will have to come back to in our sixth conversation, seems to me close to Heidegger's use of interrogation. I would locate the difference between Heidegger and you in another area, that is, in your relationship to the Judaeo-Christian tradition. I am always somewhat disturbed by what I might call the prudence with which Heidegger circumvents this tradition.

GABRIEL MARCEL: Heidegger is a Greek!

PAUL RICOEUR: It is only to the extent that your philosophy is more peri-Christian or pre-Christian than Christian that your standpoint as a philosopher of the threshold approximates Heidegger's.

GABRIEL MARCEL: Yes, probably so. I think that what Heidegger's position and my own have most fundamentally in common is the sacred sense of being, the conviction that being is a sacral reality. This seems to me extraordinarily important, and I believe it is sufficient to dispel any illusions one might have about the closeness between Heidegger and Sartre. I'm glad that you are giving me a chance to express myself on this point, because the satirical play I wrote about Heidegger could be misleading here. The French title of the play is *La Dimension fiorestan*, but the actual title is the German one, *Die Wacht am Sein*. Actually the criticism in the play is directed essentially at the use of jargon and a kind of pretension. But it doesn't exclude – and I've taken pains to say so, once in a lecture delivered at Oberhausen and another time in Berlin – it doesn't at all exclude the possibility of a metaphysical kinship between Heidegger and myself. Of course I am still a little doubtful as to how, when all is said and done, the well-known distinction between being and a being is to be interpreted. For example, I asked Henri Birault the following question: "Do you think Heidegger would accept my program of substituting for being the light, the illumining, and for a being, the illumined? Do you think Heidegger would go along with this?" Birault seemed rather skeptical. I don't know what you think of the matter. For me it's extremely important, because Heidegger's terminology is a problem for me here. I find it suspect because on the whole it depends too much on grammatical analysis. Yet it can't be denied for a moment that for Heidegger, who in certain respects is an inspired thinker, this terminology corresponds to an experience that is spiritual, speculative, and extremely deep.

PAUL RICOEUR: I would tend to minimize this disagreement about terminology and to emphasize a difference in the use of metaphor: Heidegger's metaphors are Greek, your own are biblical. [TWB, pp. 237–243]

Bibliography

Primary Sources

Marcel, Gabriel. "Existence and Objectivity," in T. Busch (ed.), *The Participant Perspective: A Gabriel Marcel Reader*. Lanham, Md.: University Press of America, 1987.

_____. *Tragic Wisdom and Beyond*, trans. S. Jolin & P. McCormick. Evanston, IL: Northwestern University Press, 1973.

_____. *Coleridge et Schelling*. Paris: Aubier, 1971.

_____. *The Philosophy of Existentialism*, trans. M. Harari. New York: Citadel, 1970.

_____. "I and Thou," trans. by F. Williams, in P. A. Schilpp and M. Friedman (eds.), *The Philosophy of Martin Buber*. LaSalle, Ill.: Open Court, 1984, 41–48.

_____. *Problematic Man*, trans. B. Thompson. New York: Herder & Herder, 1967.

_____. *Philosophical Fragments 1909–1914*, trans. L. A. Blain. Notre Dame, Ind.: Notre Dame U.P., 1965.

_____. *Searchings*. New York: Newman Press, 1964.

_____. *Creative Fidelity*, trans. R. Rosthal. New York: Farrar, Strauss, 1964. [*De refus à l'invocation*, 1940]

_____. *The Existential Background of Human Dignity*. Cambridge, Mass.: Harvard University Press, 1963.

_____. *Three Plays*. New York: Hill & Wang, 1958.

_____. *Royce's Metaphysics*, trans. V. & G. Ringer. Chicago: Regnery, 1956.

_____. *The Decline of Wisdom*, trans. M. Harari. London: Harvill Press, 1954.

_____. *Metaphysical Journal*, trans. B.Wall. London: Rockliff, 1952.

_____. *Man against Mass Society*, trans. G.S. Fraser. Chicago: Regnery, 1952 [South Bend, Ind.: St. Augustine's Press, 2008]. [*Les Hommes contre l'humain*, 1951]

_____. *Being and Having*, trans. K. Farrer. Boston: Beacon Press, 1951.

_____. *The Mystery of Being*, 2 Vols. Chicago: Regnery, 1951. Vol. I: *Reflection and Mystery*, trans. G.S. Fraser; Vol II: *Faith and Reality*, trans. R. Hague [South Bend, Ind.: St. Augustine's Press, 2001] [*Le mystère de l'être*, 1951]

_____. "Theism and Personal Relationships," *Cross Currents*, Vol. I, 1 (1950): 38–45.

_____. *Homo Viator*, trans. Emma Crauford. Chicago: Regnery, 1952 [revised, South Bend, Ind., St. Augustine's Press, 2010]. [*Homo Viator: Prolégomenes à une métaphysique de l'espérance*, 1944].

_____. *Presence and Immortality*, trans. M. Machado and revised by H.J. Koren. Pittsburgh, PA: Duquesne University Press, 1967. [also includes *Metaphysical Journal*]

_____. *Awakenings: Autobiography*, trans. P. Rogers. Milwaukee: Marquette University Press, 2002.

Secondary Sources

Anderson, T.C. "Gabriel Marcel's notions of Being," *Philosophy Today*, XIX (1975): 29–49.

_____. "Philosophy and the Experience of God according to Gabriel Marcel," *Proceedings of the Catholic Philosophical Association*, Vol. 55 (1981): 228–238.

_____. "The Nature of the Human Self according to Gabriel Marcel," *Philosophy Today*, Vol. XXIX (1985): 273–283.

_____. "The Experiential Paths to God in Kierkegaard and Marcel," *Philosophy Today*, Vol. XXVI (1982): 22–40.

Appelbaum, D. *Contact and Attention: The Anatomy of Gabriel Marcel's Metaphysical Method*. Lanham, Md.: University Press of America, 1986.

Bagot, J.P. *Connaissance et amour: essai sur la philosophie de Gabriel Marcel*. Paris: Beauchesne Press, 1958.

Benson, J. "John Wisdom and Gabriel Marcel on Proving the Existence of God," *Philosophy Today*, Vol. XXI (1987): 194–200.

Bertocci, P.A. "Descartes and Marcel on the Person and His Body: A critique," *Proceedings of the Aristotelian Society*, Vol. LXVIII (1967–68): 207–226.

Blackham, H.J. *Six Existentialist Thinkers*. London: Routledge & Kegan Paul, 1952.

Blain, L.A. "Marcel's logic of freedom in proving the existence of God," *International Philosophical Quarterly*, Vol. IX (1969): 177–204.

Bourgeois, Patrick. "Ricoeur and Marcel: An Alternative to Postmodern Deconstruction," *Bulletin de la Société Américaine de Philosophie de Langue Française*, Vol. VII (Spring 1995): 164–175.

Bugbee, R.G. "A point of co-articulation in the life and thought of Gabriel Marcel," *Philosophy Today*, Vol. XIX (1975): 61–67.

Busch, T. *Circulating Being: From Embodiment to Incorporation*. New York: Fordham University, 1999.

Cain, S. *Gabriel Marcel*. Chicago: Regnery, 1963.

_____. *Gabriel Marcel's Theory of Religious Experience*. New York: Peter Lang, 1995.

Collins, J. *The Existentialists: A Critical Study*. Chicago: Regnery, 1958.

Cooney, W. (ed.). *Contributions of Gabriel Marcel to Philosophy*. New York: Mellen Press, 1989.

Davey, M.M. *Un philosophe itinerant: Gabriel Marcel*. Paris: Flammarion, 1959.

Gallagher, K. *The Philosophy of Gabriel Marcel*. New York: Fordham U.P. 1975.

Gillman, N. *Gabriel Marcel on Religious Knowledge*. Lanham, Md.: University Press of America, 1975.

Gilson, E. "A Unique Philosopher," *Philosophy Today*, Vol. III (1959): 278–289.

———, (ed.). *Existentialisme Chretien: Gabriel Marcel*. Paris: Plon, 1947.

Godfrey, J.J. *A Philosophy of Human Hope*. Dordrecht, Martinus Nijhoff, 1987.

———. "Appraising Marcel on Hope," *Philosophy Today*, Vol.31 (1987): 234–240.

Hanley, K.R. *Dramatic Approaches to Creative Fidelity: A Study in the Theatre and Philosophy of Gabriel Marcel*. Lanham, Md.: University Press of America, 1986.

———. "Marcel: the Playwright Philosopher," *Renascence*, Vol. LV, No. 3 (Spring 2003): 241–258.

———, (ed.). *Two One Act Plays by Gabriel Marcel*. Lanham, Md.: University Press of America, 1986.

———, (ed.). *Gabriel Marcel's Perspectives on The Broken World*. Milwaukee: Marquette University Press, 1998.

———, (ed.). *Two Plays by Gabriel Marcel*. Lanham, Md.: University Press of America, 1988.

———, (ed.). *Ghostly Mysteries: A Mystery of Love And The Posthumous Joke*. Milwaukee: Marquette University Press, 2004.

Hanratty, Gerald. "The Religious Philosophy of Gabriel Marcel," *Heythrop Journal*, Vol. 17 (1976): 395–412.

Hocking, W.E. "Marcel and the Ground Issues of Metaphysics," *Philosophy and Phenomenological Research*, Vol. XIV (1954): 439–469.

Howland, M.D. *The Gift of the Other: Gabriel Marcel's Concept of Intersubjectivity in Walker Percy's Novels*. Pittsburgh: Duquesne University Press, 1990.

Keen, S. *Gabriel Marcel*. Richmond, VA: John Knox Press, 1967.

Lapointe, F.H. & C.C. *Gabriel Marcel and his Critics: An International Bibliography 1928–1977*. New York: Garland, 1977.

Lazaron, H. *Gabriel Marcel: The Dramatist*. London: Colin Smythe, 1978.

Lechner, R. "Marcel as Radical Empiricist," in P. Schilpp & L. Hahn (eds.), *The Philosophy of Gabriel Marcel*. LaSalle, Ill.: Open Court, 1984, 457–469.

———, (ed.). "Gabriel Marcel," Special Issue of *Philosophy Today*, Vol. XIX (1975).

Lehrer, K. *Theory of Knowledge*. Boulder, CO: Westview Press, 1990.

Mioeli, V.P. *Ascent to Being: Gabriel Marcel's Philosophy of Communion*. Paris: Desclée de Brouwer, 1965.

Michaud, T. "Secondary Reflection and Marcelian Anthropology," *Philosophy Today*, Vol. 34 (1990): 222–228.

———, (ed.) *Gabriel Marcel and the Postmodern World*. Special Marcel issue of the *Bulletin de la Société Américaine de Philosophie de Langue Française*, Vol. VII (Spring 1995).

Moran, D. *Gabriel Marcel*. Lanham, Md.: University Press of America, 1992.

O'Malley, J.B. *The Fellowship of Being: An Essay on the concept of Person in the Philosophy of Gabriel Marcel*. The Hague: Martinus Nijhoff, 1966.

Oyler, D. "Proofs for the existence of God in Marcel's philosophy," *Modern Schoolman*, Vol. 56 (1979), 217–235.

Pax, Clyde, *An Existentialist Approach to God: A study of Gabriel Marcel.* The Hague: Martinus Nijhoff, 1972.

_____. "Philosophical reflection: Gabriel Marcel," *The New Scholasticism*, Vol. XXXVIII (1964): 159–177.

Peccorini, F.L. *Selfhood as Thinking Thought in the work of Gabriel Marcel: A New Interpretation.* New York: Mellon Press, 1987.

Prini, P. *Gabriel Marcel et la methodologie de l'inverifiable.* Paris: Desclée de Brouwer, 1953.

Randall, A. *The Mystery of Hope in the Philosophy of Gabriel Marcel.* New York: Mellen Press, 1992

Reed, Teresa. "Aspects of Marcel's Essays," *Renascence*, Vol. LV, No. 3 (Spring 2003): 211–227.

Ricoeur, P. *Gabriel Marcel et Karl Jaspers: Philosophie du mystere et philosophie de paradox.* Paris: Editions du Temps Present, 1947.

Schilpp, P. & Hahn, L. (eds.) *The Philosophy of Gabriel Marcel.* La Salle, Ill.: Open Court, 1984.

Stallknecht, N.P. "Gabriel Marcel and the human situation," *Review of Metaphysics*, Vol. VII (1954): 661–667.

Sweetman, Brendan. *The Vision of Gabriel Marcel: Epistemology, Human Person, the Transcendent.* Amsterdam: Rodopi Press, 2008.

_____. "Marcel on God and Religious Experience, and the critique of Alston and Hick," *American Catholic Philosophical Quarterly*, Vol. 80, No.3 (Summer 2005), 407–420.

_____. "Lyotard, Postmodernism and Religion," *Philosophia Christi*, Vol.7, No. 1 (Spring 2005): 141–153.

_____. "A Rational Approach to Religious Belief," in Curtis L. Hancock and Brendan Sweetman (eds), *Faith and the Life of the Intellect.* Washington, D.C. AMA/Catholic University of America Press, 2003, 19–39.

_____. "Marcel and Phenomenology: Can Literature help Philosophy?" *Renascence*, Vol.LV, No.3 (Spring 2003): 179–192.

_____. "Gabriel Marcel: Ethics within a Christian Existentialism," in Lester Embree and John Drummond (eds.), *Phenomenological Approaches to Moral Philosophy.* Dordrecht, Netherlands: Kluwer Academic Publishers, 2002, 269–288.

_____. "Martin Buber's Epistemology," *International Philosophical Quarterly*, Vol.XLI, No.2 (June 2001): 145–160.

_____. "Postmodernism, Derrida and *Différance*: A Critique," *International Philosophical Quarterly* Vol.XXXIX, No.1 (March 1999): 5–18.

_____. "The Deconstruction of Western Metaphysics: Derrida and Maritain on Identity," in Roman Ciapalo (ed.), *Postmodernism and Christian Philosophy.* Washington, D.C.: AMA/Catholic University of America Press, 1997, 230–247.

_____. "Gabriel Marcel and the Problem of Knowledge," *Journal of the American Society for the Study of French Philosophy*, Vol.VII. No. 1–2 (Spring 1995): 148–163.

_____. "Non-conceptual knowledge in Jacques Maritain and Gabriel Marcel," in C.L. Hancock & A.O. Simon (eds.), *Freedom, Virtue, and the Common Good.* South Bend, IN: University of Notre Dame, 1995, 40–58.

_____. "Gabriel Marcel," in Trevor Hart (ed.), *Dictionary of Historical Theology.* Grand Rapids, MI: Eerdmans, 2000.

_____. "Gabriel Marcel" in Polskie Towarzystwo & Thomasza z Akwinur (eds.), *Universal Encyclopedia of Philosophy* (published in Polish and English), Vol.8. Lublin, Poland: Polish Thomas Aquinas Association, 2005, 808–812.

Traub, D.F. *Toward a Fraternal Society: A study of Gabriel Marcel's Approach to Being, Technology, and Intersubjectivity.* New York: Peter Lang, 1988.

Troisfontaines, R. *De l'existence à l'être*, Two Vols. Paris: Vrin, 1953.

Wahl, J. "Freedom and existence in some recent philosophies," *Philosophy & Phenomenological Research*, Vol. VIII (1947): 538–556.

Index

ABOUT THE EDITOR

Brendan Sweetman, a native of Dublin, Ireland, is Professor of Philosophy at Rockhurst University, Kansas City, MO, USA. He is the author or editor of many books including *The Vision of Gabriel Marcel: Epistemology, Human Person, the Transcendent* (Rodopi Press, 2008), *Religion and Science: An Introduction* (Continuum Books, 2009), *Why Politics Needs Religion: The Place of Religious Arguments in the Public Square* (InterVarsity, 2006) and *Religion: Key Concepts in Philosophy* (Continuum Books, 2007). Professor Sweetman has published more than seventy articles and reviews in a variety of journals and collections, including *International Philosophical Quarterly, American Catholic Philosophical Quarterly, Faith and Philosophy, Philosophia Christi, and Review of Metaphysics*. He writes regularly in the areas of continental philosophy, philosophy of religion, political philosophy and ethics.